THE ART OF EMOTIONAL INTELLIGENCE

*Master Your Emotions, Expand
Your Social Skills & Relationships
Abilities. Elevate Mind Power,
EQ & Embrace Happiness*

Ida Hardy

TABLE OF CONTENT

Chapter 4
Master Negative Emotions

Chapter 5
Emotional Intelligence in Relationships 65

Chapter 6
Emotional Intelligence at Work 85

Chapter 7
Case Studies 101

INTRODUCTION

In the intricate tapestry of human capabilities, one thread has increasingly asserted its vivid hue against the broader weave of skills: Emotional Intelligence (EQ). This book embarks on a journey to explore and illuminate the essence of EQ, the unique quality that enables us to engage with the complexities of our relationships - both with ourselves and others - through patience, insight, and imagination. The pages within promise to unpack the manifold facets of EQ, a form of intelligence that, despite its profound implications, has yet to claim its rightful place in the pantheon of human virtues.

Intelligence, as traditionally conceived, is often seen as a monolith, a singular beam of cognitive might that can be directed, undifferentiated, at any challenge. Yet, experience teaches us that intelligence is multifarious. A person may excel in the logical rigors of mathematics or the persuasive eloquence of language, may possess a keen acumen for business or a deft hand in technical affairs. But such prowess may coexist with personal tumult or an inner desolation, hinting at a lacuna in what we shall define as emotional intelligence.

At the heart of social dynamics, emotional intelligence is the subtle, often unnoticed force that shapes our interactions. It is the ability to sense the emotional undercurrents of those around us, to comprehend the unspoken, and to act with a discernment that transcends the obvious. It allows us to decipher the language of emotions - reading a colleague's silence as a cry for inclusion, interpreting a partner's irritability as a masked appeal for support.

Turning inward, emotional intelligence manifests as a considered skepticism toward our immediate emotions. It recognizes that our most visceral reactions - love, desire, anger, envy - may not always steer us true. The emotionally intelligent individual harbors no blind trust in the gut but questions where these emotions stem from, how they are entwined with our past, and how they might misguide us. It is a shield against the siren songs of our impulses, a lens to better understand our deepest drives.

This intelligence is the ally of those who face life's vicissitudes not with fragility but with a somber, sometimes darkly humorous, resilience. It is the quality that allows one to meet defeat with a knowing smile, to recognize that a well-tempered pessimism can be a companion to hope, guiding us through the thicket of existence with a realistic yet unbroken spirit.

Contrary to what one might think, emotional intelligence is not a fixed trait, dispensed by the whims of nature in unequal measure. It is a learned skill, a mosaic of understanding pieced together through education and reflection. Ideally, it would be the cornerstone of our formative years, infused into the curriculum alongside arithmetic and literature, sculpting minds adept not only at navigating the world but also at understanding the human condition.

Yet, our progress in technical intelligence - a force that has seen us subjugate nature and bend the world to our will - has not been matched by advancements in emotional wisdom. The dissonance between our technological prowess and emotional maturity is stark, presenting a danger of the highest order. We stand as sophisticated beings armed with the tools of gods, yet hamstrung by the emotional acumen of our primal ancestors.

This book posits that the very fate of our civilization hinges on a collective mastery of emotional intelligence. And this mastery must extend beyond the confines of formal education; it must permeate our culture in all its expressions. Every tragedy and comedy, every song and story, every edifice and digital creation can be a conduit for lessons in EQ, a means to inculcate the sensibilities that make us truly human.

In the pages that follow, we embark on a vital mission: to understand the intricacies of emotional intelligence and to harness its potential. As we navigate through the chapters, we will discover how EQ can transform our lives, foster deeper connections, and nurture a society that is both emotionally astute and profoundly wise. The future - humane, enlightened, and emotionally intelligent - beckons. Let us answer the call, while there is still time.

CHAPTER 1

WHAT IS EMOTIONAL INTELLIGENCE?

Emotional Intelligence (EQ), as coined and elaborated upon by psychologist Daniel Goleman, is a pivotal skill set encompassing the adeptness to perceive, comprehend, manage, and harness emotions both in oneself and others in a productive and adaptive fashion. It unfolds a wide spectrum of emotional and social skills that are instrumental in navigating through life's hurdles, nurturing meaningful connections, and enhancing personal and professional pursuits.

At the core of Emotional Intelligence lie five cardinal components as outlined by Goleman, who is a distinguished figure in the domain of Emotional Quotient (EQ):

1. Self-awareness: This is the foundational step where individuals become cognizant of their own emotions, strengths, weaknesses, values, and motives, along with understanding how these elements resonate with others. Being self-aware illuminates the correlation between one's emotions, thoughts, and actions, and how these, in turn, reverberate through the surrounding environment and relationships.

2. Self-regulation: This component encapsulates the capacity to manage one's emotions proficiently, particularly in stressful or challenging scenarios, ensuring they don't hinder personal or interpersonal functioning. It also entails a readiness to adapt to changes and a proactiveness to seize the initiative as situations warrant.

3. Motivation: Here, individuals harness an intrinsic drive to achieve their aspirations, marked by a robust commitment and an optimistic outlook even in the face of setbacks. This motivational facet of EQ propels individuals to pursue goals with energy and persistence.

4. Empathy (Social Awareness): This is about tuning into the emotional undercurrents of others, comprehending their perspectives, and fostering a supportive network of relationships. Empathy extends into organizational awareness, aiding in deciphering social complexities within group dynamics.

5. Social Skills (Relationship Management): This component embodies the expertise to inspire, influence, and nurture development in others while adeptly managing conflicts. It's about honing the ability to communicate effectively, foster rewarding relationships, and navigate through social intricacies.

The emergence of Emotional Intelligence as a concept in the 1990s, with Goleman at the helm, although grounded in the earlier work of researchers Peter Salovey and John D. Mayer, has been monumental. Their initial framework defined Emotional Intelligence as the capability to monitor and discern one's own and others' emotions, utilizing this awareness to steer one's thoughts and actions.

The philosophy of Emotional Intelligence suggests a departure from the static nature of IQ, proposing EQ as a malleable skill set subject to development and refinement over time. This perspective has been a watershed in the realms of personal development and organizational psychology, advocating the potential for individuals and collectives to foster superior emotional insight and management, thereby achieving improved outcomes.

In the ensuing years, the discourse on Emotional Intelligence has matured, with various models and frameworks like the Bar-On Model of Emotional-Social Intelligence and the Trait Emotional Intelligence framework emerging to offer more granular insights into the myriad emotional and social competencies, skills, and behaviors that underpin intelligent behavior.

The narrative of Emotional Intelligence has morphed over time, now encapsulating a more intricate understanding of emotional and social competencies. The diverse nature of EQ underscores the intricacy of human emotions and the multitude of ways they intersect with cognition, behavior, decision-making, relationships, and overall life experiences.

To encapsulate, Emotional Intelligence transcends being merely "emotionally smart"; it's about leveraging emotions to augment our life quality, engage optimally with others, and navigate life's challenges and opportunities adeptly. It underscores the delicate balance and symbiotic interplay between our emotional and cognitive faculties, fostering a life replete with balance, success, and fulfillment.

IMPORTANCE OF EMOTIONAL INTELLIGENCE

Emotional Intelligence (EQ) holds significant value in enhancing personal and interpersonal experiences in life. Its relevance is wide-reaching, affecting personal development, professional growth, and social interactions. Here's a more detailed elaboration on the importance of Emotional Intelligence:

PERSONAL GROWTH:

- **Self-Understanding:** Through EQ, individuals can achieve a better understanding of their emotions, strengths, and weaknesses, fostering a sense of self-acceptance and a proactive mindset towards self-improvement.

- **Resilience:** Higher levels of emotional intelligence contribute to greater resilience, aiding individuals in managing their emotions effectively during challenging times, thereby facilitating recovery from adversities.

INTERPERSONAL RELATIONSHIPS:

- **Empathy:** By nurturing empathy, EQ enables individuals to understand and share the feelings of others, which is crucial for building meaningful and lasting relationships.

- **Conflict Resolution:** Effective conflict resolution is often rooted in EQ, as understanding and managing personal and others' emotions are vital for finding common ground and resolving disputes amicably.

- Attraction and Rapport: Emotional intelligence plays a significant role in the realm of seduction and rules of attraction. Being attuned to one's own emotions and the emotions of others facilitates the building of attraction and rapport. Understanding and responding to verbal and non-verbal cues can create a connection and a sense of intimacy.

- Authenticity and Respect: EQ promotes authenticity and respect in interactions, which are vital for creating a genuine and meaningful connection, rather than a superficial or manipulative interaction.

PROFESSIONAL SUCCESS:

- Teamwork and Collaboration: The ability to work well in teams and collaborative settings is often reflective of one's emotional intelligence. EQ fosters a respectful and understanding environment, conducive to achieving collective goals.

- Leadership: Many leadership qualities like inspiring and motivating others, managing conflict, and navigating organizational change, are closely tied to EQ. Effective leaders often exhibit high levels of emotional intelligence, guiding their teams successfully through the complex dynamics of the modern workplace.

DECISION MAKING:

- Impulse Control: EQ aids in controlling impulses and avoiding hasty decisions, allowing for more sound and well-considered decision-making.

- Problem-Solving: Emotionally intelligent individuals are better equipped to maintain a clear mind and stay objective in challenging situations, which is conducive to effective problem-solving.

HEALTH AND WELL-BEING:

- Stress Management: Managing emotions effectively is key to coping with stress, reducing anxiety, and promoting mental well-being. EQ provides the tools for managing emotional responses to stressors, thereby promoting a balanced and healthy life.

- Happiness: There's a strong correlation between emotional intelligence and happiness. The skills associated with EQ contribute to an overall higher level of life satisfaction.

SOCIETAL IMPACT:

- Social Cohesion: Emotional intelligence promotes tolerance, understanding, and mutual respect among different societal groups, fostering social cohesion and harmonious coexistence.

LIFELONG LEARNING:

- Adaptability: Emotional intelligence fosters adaptability, an essential skill in our rapidly evolving world. Individuals with higher EQ are often more open to new experiences and can adjust more easily to changing circumstances.

The importance of Emotional Intelligence is profound and enduring, transcending individual benefits to contribute to healthier, more harmonious relationships and communities. Its cultivation is an investment towards a more fulfilling, successful, and meaningful life.

HISTORICAL OVERVIEW

The roots of Emotional Intelligence can be traced back to early psychological theories, though the term itself wasn't coined until the 20th century. This is just an overview in order to know the different phases of the EQ evolution.

Below is a step-by-step traversal through the timeline of how Emotional Intelligence emerged and evolved:

EARLY 20TH CENTURY:

- Psychological Foundations: Early in the 20th century, psychologists began exploring emotions and their impact on behavior and cognition. However, these were largely isolated inquiries rather than a consolidated exploration of emotional intelligence as a concept.

1975 - Howard Gardner's Theory:

- Multiple Intelligences: Psychologist Howard Gardner introduced the theory of multiple intelligences in 1975, which included interpersonal and intrapersonal intelligences. This was a stepping stone towards recognizing emotional intelligence as a distinct form of intelligence.

1983 - Daniel Goleman's Seminal Work:

- Popularization: Daniel Goleman is often credited with popularizing the concept of emotional intelligence with his 1995 book "Emotional Intelligence: Why It Can Matter More Than IQ." Goleman's work brought the term into the mainstream, emphasizing its importance in everyday life and the workplace.

LATE 20TH CENTURY:

- Models of EQ: Following Goleman's work, different models of emotional intelligence emerged. These include the ability model by Peter Salovey and John D. Mayer, which focuses on the individual's ability to process emotional information, and Goleman's mixed model, which combines emotional abilities with interpersonal skills and personal qualities.

EARLY 21ST CENTURY:

- **Further Research:** The early 2000s saw a significant increase in research on emotional intelligence, leading to a more nuanced understanding of its components and its impact on various areas of life including leadership, education, and mental health.

DEVELOPMENT OF ASSESSMENTS:

- **Measurement:** With the growing interest in emotional intelligence, various assessment tools were developed to measure EQ, including the Emotional Intelligence Appraisal, the Bar-On Emotional Quotient Inventory (EQ-i), and the Mayer-Salovey-Caruso Emotional Intelligence Test (MSCEQT).

INTEGRATION IN CORPORATE AND EDUCATIONAL SECTORS:

- **Application:** The recognition of the importance of emotional intelligence has led to its integration in corporate training programs and educational curricula to enhance interpersonal skills, leadership, and personal development.

ONGOING EVOLUTION:

- **Modern Understanding:** The understanding of emotional intelligence continues to evolve with ongoing research. Current exploration delves into the neuroscientific basis of emotional intelligence, its impact on leadership efficacy, team performance, and its role in the broader societal context.

The journey of emotional intelligence from a vaguely defined concept to a well-recognized and highly valued field reflects a growing acknowledgment of the significance of emotions in our personal, social, and professional lives. The historical evolution of Emotional Intelligence not only sheds light on the development of the concept but also paves the way for future research and applications aimed at harnessing the power of emotional intelligence for individual and collective betterment.

EMOTIONAL INTELLIGENCE MODELS & COMPARISON WITH OTHER TYPES OF INTELLIGENCE

Emotional Intelligence (EQ) represents a paradigm shift in the understanding of intelligence. Unlike traditional IQ, which quantifies cognitive abilities, EI models emphasize the ability to perceive, control, and evaluate emotions. This form of intelligence is crucial in navigating social complexities and making personal decisions that achieve positive results. Various models of EI offer different perspectives and components. Comparing EQ to other intelligences like spatial or logical-mathematical, highlights its unique contribution to how we understand success and interpersonal dynamics in both personal and professional realms. Below listed the existing models:

MAYER AND SALOVEY MODEL (1997):

- **Four-Branch Model:** This model posits Emotional Intelligence as a set of four related abilities: perceiving emotions, using emotions to facilitate thought, understanding emotions, and managing emotions. Each of these abilities represents a different stage in the processing of emotional information.

GOLEMAN'S MIXED MODEL (1995):

- **Five Components:** Daniel Goleman's model proposes EQ as a mix of abilities and traits, encompassing self-awareness, self-regulation, motivation, empathy, and social skills. It's termed a 'mixed' model as it combines emotional abilities with personal and social competencies.

BAR-ON MODEL OF EMOTIONAL-SOCIAL INTELLIGENCE (ESI) (1997):

- **Five Meta-Factors:** Reuven Bar-On's model views Emotional Intelligence as a cross-section of interrelated emotional and social competencies, skills, and facilitators that impact intelligent behavior. This model comprises five meta-factors including intrapersonal skills, interpersonal skills, stress management, adaptability, and general mood.

TRAIT EMOTIONAL INTELLIGENCE MODEL (2001):

- **Emotional Self-Efficacy:** Proposed by K.V. Petrides, this model treats EQ as a collection of emotional self-perceptions located at the lower levels of personality. It's focused on the individual's self-perceived abilities and traits related to emotional understanding and expression.

GENOS MODEL (2002):

- **Seven Competencies:** The Genos model, developed by Dr. Ben Palmer and Dr. Gilles Gignac, focuses on emotionally intelligent workplace behavior. It identifies seven core emotional intelligence competencies, including self-awareness, emotional expression, emotional awareness of others, emotional reasoning, emotional self-management, emotional management of others, and emotional self-control.

SIX SECONDS MODEL (1997):

- **Three Pursuits:** This model introduces a process framework for making practical sense of Emotional Intelligence. It includes three pursuits: Know Yourself (building self-awareness), Choose Yourself (exercising self-management), and Give Yourself (being purposeful and contributing to others).

THE YALE MODEL:

- RULER Approach: Developed at the Yale Center for Emotional Intelligence, this model uses the acronym RULER to encompass its five skills of EQ: Recognizing, Understanding, Labeling, Expressing, and Regulating emotions. This model is often utilized in educational settings to teach EQ. Each of these models provides a unique lens through which to understand and apply Emotional Intelligence, whether in personal, social, or professional contexts. They collectively contribute to a robust and multifaceted understanding of Emotional Intelligence, elucidating the intricate interplay of emotions, cognitive processes, and behaviors that shape our interactions with ourselves and the world around us. Through these models, practitioners, educators, and individuals can access a rich toolkit for developing and enhancing Emotional Intelligence, fostering personal growth, and improving interpersonal relationships. We're going to focus on Goleman's model as reference for this book.

Furthermore let's focus on a short comparison with other forms of Intelligence:

COGNITIVE INTELLIGENCE (IQ):

- Nature: Cognitive intelligence primarily refers to abilities such as memory, problem-solving, and analytical skills, which are often quantified through Intelligence Quotient (IQ) tests.

- Static vs Dynamic: Unlike EQ, IQ remains relatively stable throughout one's life. Moreover, IQ tends to operate in a more static manner, while EQ engages dynamically with one's environment, adapting to social and emotional cues.

- Performance Indicator: While IQ is a robust predictor of academic and occupational performance, it doesn't account for interpersonal effectiveness or self-management, areas where EQ shines.

MULTIPLE INTELLIGENCES THEORY (HOWARD GARDNER):

- **Scope:** Gardner's theory posits multiple forms of intelligence, including linguistic, logical-mathematical, spatial, bodily-kinesthetic, musical, interpersonal, intrapersonal, and naturalistic intelligence. EQ overlaps with Gardner's interpersonal and intrapersonal intelligences.

- **Holistic Understanding:** Unlike the narrow focus of IQ, both Multiple Intelligences and EQ strive for a more holistic understanding of human capability, recognizing the importance of social and self-awareness.

PRACTICAL INTELLIGENCE (ROBERT STERNBERG):

- **Real-world Problem Solving:** Practical intelligence concerns the ability to solve real-world problems and adapt to change. Like EQ, it values the importance of context and real-world effectiveness over abstract reasoning.

- **Contextual Engagement:** Both practical intelligence and EQ emphasize engaging with one's environment in a meaningful, effective manner, although EQ specifically focuses on the emotional and social dimensions.

CREATIVE INTELLIGENCE:

- **Innovation and Imagination:** Creative intelligence is about innovative thinking and the ability to generate original ideas. While it doesn't directly overlap with EQ, emotionally intelligent individuals may foster a conducive environment for creativity by managing emotions and social dynamics effectively.

- **Complementarity:** Creative and emotional intelligences can complement each other, enhancing problem-solving, decision-making, and interpersonal relationships in diverse settings.

MORAL INTELLIGENCE:

- Ethical Understanding: Moral intelligence entails the ability to discern right from wrong and adhere to ethical principles. EQ can contribute to moral intelligence by fostering empathy, understanding, and respect in interpersonal interactions.

KINESTHETIC INTELLIGENCE:

- Physical Mastery: This form of intelligence is related to physical activities and mastery over one's body movements. While distinct, EQ can enhance kinesthetic intelligence by aiding in stress management, focus, and teamwork in physically demanding settings.

SOCIAL INTELLIGENCE:

- Overlap: Social Intelligence and EQ share substantial overlap, with both focusing on understanding and navigating social situations. However, EQ delves deeper into managing one's own emotions and those of others.

In essence, Emotional Intelligence bridges the gap between cognitive capabilities and human emotions, offering a balanced framework to navigate complex social landscapes. It complements other forms of intelligence, contributing to a richer, more holistic understanding of human capability and performance across a multitude of domains.

CHAPTER 2

COMPONENTS OF EMOTIONAL INTELLIGENCE

As we embark on a profound exploration of Emotional Intelligence (EQ), this chapter serves as a critical juncture, illuminating the five core components that form the foundation of EQ as introduced by Daniel Goleman. These components are not just abstract concepts; they are the essential building blocks that shape our interactions, guide our personal growth, and influence our success in life.

Self-awareness, the first component, is akin to the intimate knowledge of one's inner world, an acute understanding of one's emotions, triggers, and inner compass. It is the mirror through which we can objectively observe our true selves. Self-regulation, the second, is the mastery of one's emotional responses, the ability to navigate through storms with composure and deliberate actions. Motivation, the third, is the internal engine that drives us to pursue goals with passion and resilience, beyond external rewards or recognition.

The fourth component, empathy, is the bridge that connects us to others, allowing us to perceive and understand the emotional landscapes of those around us. And finally, social skills – the fifth component – are the tools we use to navigate, negotiate, and nurture the relationships that we build, making them both meaningful and productive.

Throughout this chapter, we will dissect each component, delving into their individual nuances and the synergistic effects they create when combined. By understanding and cultivating these components, we can aspire to not only better ourselves but also to enhance the quality of our collective human experience. Join me as we unpack these pillars of Emotional Intelligence, one by one, learning how to integrate them into the fabric of our daily lives.

SELF-AWARENESS:

Self-Awareness is a pivotal facet of Emotional Intelligence (EQ), serving as the cornerstone for cultivating an enriched understanding of oneself and others. It entails a profound comprehension of one's emotions, strengths, weaknesses, values, and motivational drives. By fostering self-awareness, individuals can gauge the extensive impact of their emotions, not only on their thought processes but also on their actions and interactions.

The significance of self-awareness transcends personal realization; it is the bedrock upon which other EQ components are built. For instance, without recognizing one's emotional triggers or understanding personal values, the ability to manage emotions (self-regulation) could be compromised. Similarly, an enhanced self-awareness fosters empathetic understanding and improved social interactions, thereby bolstering other EQ domains like empathy and social skills.

To nurture self-awareness, several practical steps can be undertaken. Mindfulness meditation and reflective practices are potent tools that encourage individuals to delve into their emotional states and underlying beliefs. Keeping a journal to track emotions, reactions, and daily experiences can also provide insightful revelations about personal emotional patterns. Furthermore, soliciting feedback from trusted peers or mentors can unveil blind spots and offer a more rounded self-perception. Engaging in personality assessments or emotional intelligence tests can also furnish individuals with a structured understanding of their emotional landscape.

Through a combination of reflective practices, feedback, and assessments, individuals can significantly enhance their self-awareness, laying a robust foundation for developing other emotional intelligence competencies. This holistic approach not only contributes to personal growth but also paves the way for enriched relationships and a gratifying life journey.

SELF-REGULATION:

Self-Regulation stands at the core of Emotional Intelligence as the capacity to master one's emotional responses, particularly in high-pressure scenarios, and to remain flexible in the face of change. It's a dynamic process involving emotional self-control, conscientiousness, and an ability to adapt strategies to suit shifting circumstances.

The role of self-regulation in achieving personal and professional success is immense. It enables individuals to maintain composure, think clearly, and make decisions without the clouding influence of transient emotions. In the workplace, self-regulation is linked to higher productivity and better interpersonal dynamics. It is equally vital in personal realms, as it aids in coping with adversity, thus leading to improved mental health and well-being.

Improving self-regulation can be approached through several practical techniques. Mindfulness exercises, such as focused breathing and sensory observation, train the mind to remain anchored in the present, reducing impulsivity. Developing coping strategies in advance for known stressors - such as preparation and rehearsal - can mitigate emotional upheaval. Setting clear personal standards and values helps guide behavior consistently, rather than reacting to each moment. Furthermore, cultivating an optimistic outlook enables adaptability, allowing individuals to view challenges as opportunities rather than threats.

Strengthening self-regulation is not an overnight task; it requires persistent effort and self-reflection. However, the benefits of such development are far-reaching, equipping individuals with the fortitude to navigate the complexities of life with grace and resilience.

MOTIVATION:

Motivation in the context of Emotional Intelligence (EQ) is the internal engine that propels individuals toward their goals, not for external rewards, but for the fulfillment and satisfaction derived from the achievement itself. This intrinsic form of motivation is characterized by a deep-seated passion and a persistent drive to pursue personal and organizational objectives, with enthusiasm that is both infectious and inspiring.

The importance of motivation in achieving personal and professional objectives cannot be overstated. It is the motivating force that fuels persistence in the face of setbacks and energizes individuals to push the boundaries of their capabilities. In a professional setting, a highly motivated individual often stands out for their commitment to excellence, driving not only their own success but also galvanizing the collective momentum of their team or organization.

Fostering intrinsic motivation can be achieved through various strategies. Firstly, setting challenging yet attainable goals can provide a clear direction and a sense of purpose. Regularly revisiting and refining these goals ensures they remain aligned with personal values and professional growth. Secondly, cultivating an environment that encourages autonomy and provides opportunities for skill mastery can significantly enhance intrinsic motivation. Individuals are more driven when they feel they have control over their work and can see themselves progressing towards expertise.

Another effective approach is to focus on the enjoyment and learning aspect of tasks rather than solely on the outcome. This perspective helps maintain enthusiasm even during mundane or difficult projects. Additionally, providing and seeking feedback helps individuals understand the impact of their work, reinforcing their sense of purpose.

Lastly, surrounding oneself with supportive peers and mentors can also stimulate motivation. The energy and ideas of passionate individuals are often contagious, creating a dynamic and motivating atmosphere.

In essence, motivation is a key pillar of EQ, acting as a catalyst for sustained personal growth and professional excellence. It's a deeply personal yet universally essential component, integral for anyone aiming to live a driven and purposeful life.

EMPATHY:

Empathy, a central tenet of Emotional Intelligence (EQ), is the capacity to understand and share the feelings of others. It goes beyond mere sympathy, extending into a genuine understanding of and concern for the emotional states of those around us. This emotional resonance is not just about feeling what others feel but involves a cognitive component that compels one to acknowledge and consider another's perspective.

The role of empathy in forging and sustaining successful relationships is monumental. It acts as a relational glue that connects people on a deeper level, fostering trust and open communication. In professional contexts, empathy contributes to building strong teams where members feel understood and valued, leading to increased collaboration and productivity. In personal relationships, it deepens bonds and facilitates more meaningful connections.

Developing empathic skills can be approached through a variety of exercises. One effective practice is active listening, which involves giving full attention to the speaker, acknowledging their feelings, and providing feedback that shows understanding. This technique requires the listener to refrain from judgment and to focus on the speaker's emotions and underlying messages.

Another exercise is to engage in role reversal or perspective-taking, where one attempts to view situations from the point of view of another person. This can be done through reflective journaling or imaginative scenarios, which help to cultivate an understanding of the complexities of others' experiences.

Practicing mindfulness is also beneficial for enhancing empathy. Mindfulness meditation focuses on being present and aware, which can heighten one's ability to detect and respond to the emotional states of others. By being more attuned to the present moment, individuals can better perceive the subtle nonverbal cues that are critical to empathetic understanding.

Lastly, exposing oneself to diverse situations and people can broaden one's empathetic range. By stepping out of one's comfort zone and interacting with a wide array of individuals, one can gain insight into different life experiences and viewpoints, which in turn nurtures a more empathetic outlook.

In sum, empathy is a dynamic skill that can be cultivated and refined. Its significance lies in its ability to bridge emotional gaps, enabling individuals to build robust, compassionate, and understanding relationships across personal and professional spheres.

SOCIAL SKILLS:

Social skills in the context of Emotional Intelligence (EQ) encompass the adeptness to manage and navigate relationships, build networks, and identify commonalities that forge connections. These skills are instrumental in cultivating a collaborative environment, resolving conflicts amicably, and establishing effective leadership.

In collaboration, social skills are the driving force that brings individuals together to work towards a shared goal. They enable team members to communicate effectively, respect one another's viewpoints, and contribute constructively. The ability to listen, provide feedback, and motivate others is pivotal in maintaining a cooperative team dynamic. Social skills ensure that collaboration is not just a group effort but a synergistic one, where the sum is greater than its parts.

Conflict resolution greatly benefits from strong social skills. The capacity to manage emotions, recognize the emotional states of others, and engage in active listening contributes to resolving disputes with empathy and understanding. Skilled individuals can de-escalate tense situations, negotiate solutions, and mediate discussions to reach a consensus. They also know when to compromise and when to stand firm, balancing assertiveness with flexibility.

Leadership is profoundly influenced by one's social skills. Leaders with high EQ are adept at inspiring and guiding teams, communicating vision, and leading by example. They build trust and rapport, fostering an environment where feedback is encouraged and valued. Their ability to connect with team members on an emotional level enhances their influence and ability to drive performance.

Improving social skills can be a deliberate and strategic endeavor. Here are some tips & examples for enhancing interpersonal skills and relationship management – several of these aspects will be covered within the following chapters -:

Active Listening: Practice fully concentrating on the speaker, understanding their message, responding thoughtfully, and remembering the conversation. This shows respect and value for their input.

Effective Communication: Be clear and articulate in expressing thoughts and expectations. Tailor the message to the audience and ensure it is received and understood.

Feedback Loop: Learn to give and receive feedback graciously. Constructive criticism can be a powerful tool for growth when delivered appropriately.

Conflict Navigation: Develop strategies for conflict resolution that focus on the issue rather than the person. Strive to understand the underlying issues and work towards a mutually beneficial resolution.

Empathy in Action: Show genuine concern for others' needs and feelings. This builds deeper, more meaningful connections.

Building Rapport: Take an interest in people, remember details about them, and find common interests. This establishes a foundation for positive interactions.

Networking: Engage with a diverse range of individuals. Broad networks can provide support, insight, and opportunities.

Adaptability: Be open to change and different viewpoints. Adaptability is key to navigating the social landscape effectively.

Cultural Sensitivity: Be aware of and respectful towards different cultures, practices, and norms. This awareness is crucial in today's globalized environment.

Inspirational Influence: Positively motivate and influence others. Authentic enthusiasm is contagious and can inspire teams to achieve collective goals.

By honing these social skills, individuals can strengthen their relationships, enhance their leadership capabilities, and contribute to a more productive and harmonious work environment.

Each component is explored in a dedicated section, commencing with a theoretical explanation followed by real-life examples that illustrate the significance of the particular EQ component.

The aim of this structured exploration is to provide readers with a comprehensive understanding of Emotional Intelligence's components, enabling them to recognize the impact of emotions on their thoughts, behaviors, and interactions with others. Through theoretical insights and practical exercises, you are guided on a path to enhancing your EQ, which in turn, can significantly contribute to improving your quality of life, both personally and professionally.

CHAPTER 3

PREPARE YOURSELF: IMPROVING EMOTIONAL INTELLIGENCE

In the journey of personal growth and professional development, the mastery of emotional intelligence (EQ) stands as a beacon, guiding individuals through the complexities of human interaction and self-understanding. This chapter is crafted as a transformative passage towards heightened self-regulation, refined self-awareness, and enriched motivation.

As we embark on this path, we recognize that the ability to enhance self-regulation is not just about controlling impulses or managing stress in the moment; it is about setting the stage for sustained success and well-being. We delve into practical strategies that help us navigate our emotional landscape with finesse, turning potential upheavals into moments of clarity and growth.

Developing self-awareness, the cornerstone of EQ, invites us to hold up a mirror to our inner workings, to understand the 'why' behind our emotions, and to appreciate the strengths and vulnerabilities that shape our decisions. Through this deepened self-knowledge, we gain the power to act with intention rather than react out of habit.

Finally, fostering motivation transcends the superficial layers of external rewards to tap into the wellspring of intrinsic motivation. It is here that we uncover our deepest drives and passions, fueling our journey with purpose and perseverance.

Each section of this chapter presents a tapestry of insights and exercises designed to enhance your emotional intelligence. By engaging with these practices, you equip yourself with invaluable tools for personal refinement and professional excellence. Welcome to a transformative process that not only prepares you for the challenges ahead but also enriches your entire human experience.

DEVELOPING SELF-AWARENESS

Developing self-awareness is a transformative process that uncovers the core of who we are, including our emotions, strengths, weaknesses, and deep-seated values. This chapter will guide you through practical strategies to cultivate a profound understanding of your inner self, which is essential for personal growth and the effective application of emotional intelligence.

INTROSPECTION: THE INNER DIALOGUE

Initiating regular introspection is the cornerstone of self-awareness. Dedicate time each day to reflect on your thoughts, feelings, and behaviors. This can be done through quiet contemplation, meditation, or writing in a journal.

Carve out a few minutes each day for introspection. This could be during your morning coffee, a quiet moment before bed, or even during a daily walk. Reflect on your day: What emotions surfaced and why? How did you respond to various situations? What emotions did I feel today? What caused these emotions? How did I react? Why did I react that way? This regular practice can be as simple as thinking quietly or jotting down thoughts in a notebook or digital app.

EMOTIONAL LITERACY: NAMING YOUR FEELINGS

Increasing your emotional literacy is about being able to identify and label your emotions correctly. It's more nuanced than simply stating you're happy or sad. Are you content, elated, or hopeful? Are you disappointed, grieving, or discouraged? Enhancing your emotional vocabulary allows for a more accurate understanding of your emotional state.

FEEDBACK: THE MIRROR OTHERS HOLD UP

Seeking feedback from trusted individuals in your life is a powerful way to gain insight into how you are perceived by others. It can highlight discrepancies between your self-perception and the impact you have on those around you. Be open to receiving this feedback, and consider it objectively, without defensiveness.

PERSONALITY ASSESSMENTS: TOOLS FOR SELF-DISCOVERY

Engage with reputable personality assessments to gain a structured understanding of your character traits. Instruments like the Myers-Briggs Type Indicator or the Enneagram can provide a framework for understanding your behavioral tendencies, motivations, and ways of interacting with the world.

Example: How to use Personality Assessments in a practical way.

Situation: Sarah, a 30-year-old marketing manager, often finds herself struggling with team dynamics at work. She feels that her ideas are not always understood or appreciated, leading to frustration and decreased job satisfaction.

ACTION:

Sarah learns about the Myers-Briggs Type Indicator (MBTI), which categorizes individuals into 16 personality types based on preferences in four areas: Introversion/Extraversion, Sensing/Intuition, Thinking/Feeling, and Judging/Perceiving.

Sarah decides to take the MBTI test online. The results show that she is an INFJ (Introverted, Intuitive, Feeling, Judging). The description indicates that she prefers to work in a structured way, is highly intuitive about people, and often puts the needs of others above her own.

REFLECTION:

Sarah reflects on these results. She realizes that her preference for structure might clash with more spontaneous colleagues. Her intuition about others' feelings could be why she feels deeply affected by team dynamics.

Curious about more perspectives, Sarah also takes the Enneagram test, which identifies her as a Type 2: The Helper. This type is described as being caring, empathetic, and possessive.

Sarah begins to see patterns in her behavior. Her tendency to prioritize others' needs (a trait of both INFJ and Type 2) might explain why she sometimes feels overlooked in group settings.

With this new understanding, Sarah makes conscious efforts to assert her ideas in meetings. She also works on setting boundaries, ensuring her needs and ideas are voiced and valued.

Sarah shares her findings with her team during a team-building session. This opens a dialogue about different working styles and preferences, leading to a better understanding among team members.

OUTCOME:

- **Improved Communication:** Sarah's improved self-awareness helps her communicate her needs more effectively, leading to better collaboration.

- **Enhanced Self-Understanding:** The insights from the personality assessments empower Sarah to understand her intrinsic motivations and behaviors.

- **Team Development:** Sharing her journey inspires her colleagues to explore their own personality traits, fostering a more empathetic and cohesive team environment.

Sarah reminds herself that these personality assessments are not rigid classifications but tools to understand tendencies and preferences. She uses this knowledge not to box herself in but as a guide for personal and professional growth.

SETTING PERSONAL BOUNDARIES: KNOWING YOUR LIMITS

Understanding and setting personal boundaries is a critical aspect of self-awareness. It involves recognizing where you end and others begin, what you are comfortable with, and what you will not tolerate. Boundaries protect your sense of self and help you maintain emotional well-being.

EXPLORING YOUR VALUES AND BELIEFS

Your values and beliefs are the compass that guides your decisions and actions. Take the time to explicitly define them. What matters most to you? What principles do you stand by? When your actions are in alignment with your values, you will experience greater harmony and purpose.

PHYSICAL AWARENESS: THE BODY-MIND CONNECTION

Your body often manifests signs of your emotional state. Pay attention to physical cues, such as tension, breathing patterns, or energy levels, as they can be indicators of underlying emotions. Techniques like body scanning can help you become more attuned to these signals.

TRACKING PROGRESS: THE JOURNEY MAPPED

Document your progress in developing self-awareness. Note moments of insight, patterns that emerge, and how your self-perception evolves over time. This tracking can be a source of motivation and a reminder of how far you've come on your journey.

In conclusion, developing self-awareness is an ongoing process that requires curiosity, honesty, and a willingness to confront uncomfortable truths. By employing the strategies outlined in this chapter, you will build a solid foundation of self-knowledge, which is the first step towards mastering emotional intelligence and enhancing your interactions with the world around you.

ENHANCING SELF-REGULATION

Self-regulation is a key aspect of emotional intelligence that allows us to manage our thoughts, emotions, and behaviors in beneficial ways. It empowers us to handle stress, control impulses, and navigate through life's ups and downs with composure and clarity. This chapter delves into practical strategies for enhancing self-regulation, equipping you with the tools to maintain emotional equilibrium and pursue your goals with focus and resilience.

SETTING THE STAGE FOR SELF-CONTROL

The foundation of self-regulation lies in creating an environment that supports emotional balance. This includes establishing routines that foster stability and predictability, such as regular sleep patterns, healthy eating habits, and consistent exercise. These routines not only strengthen physical health but also bolster mental fortitude, providing a steady baseline from which to operate.

RECOGNIZING TRIGGERS AND RESPONSES

A critical step in enhancing self-regulation is to identify personal triggers - situations, people, or thoughts that elicit strong emotional responses. By acknowledging these triggers, you can anticipate and prepare for emotional reactions. Keeping a journal can be an effective way to track these triggers and your responses, offering insights into patterns that you may wish to change.

JOURNAL ENTRY EXAMPLE: IDENTIFYING AND MANAGING EMOTIONAL TRIGGERS

Date: January 5, 2023

Time: 7:45 PM

Current Mood: Anxious and a bit frustrated

Trigger Event: Today's team meeting at work. During the discussion, my idea was dismissed by a colleague, and the manager didn't acknowledge my contribution.

EMOTIONAL RESPONSE:

* Felt undervalued and angry.
* My heart rate increased, and I could feel my face getting hot.
* Experienced a strong urge to retaliate verbally.

THOUGHTS DURING THE EVENT:

* Why don't they ever listen to my ideas?
* I feel disrespected and ignored.
* Maybe my ideas aren't good enough.

PHYSICAL SENSATIONS:

* Tightness in chest.
* Clenched jaw.
* Shallow breathing.

BEHAVIOR FOLLOWING THE EVENT:

* Withdrew from the conversation.
* Gave short, terse responses when directly addressed.
* Didn't participate further in the meeting.

REFLECTION:

* Realizing my sensitivity to having my ideas dismissed or not being heard.
* The intensity of my reaction might be linked to past experiences of feeling overlooked.

COPING STRATEGIES USED:

* Took deep breaths to calm down.
* Reminded myself of previous successful ideas that were implemented.
* Decided not to respond immediately to avoid escalating the situation.

PLANS FOR FUTURE MANAGEMENT:

1. Preparation: Before future meetings, I will rehearse how to assertively present my ideas and how to respond calmly if they are not immediately accepted.

2. Perspective-Taking: I will try to understand the viewpoints of others and remind myself that disagreement is not a personal attack.

3. Self-Care Post-Event: Engage in a calming activity after such meetings, like a short walk or listening to music, to reset my emotional state.

4. Seek Feedback: I will discuss this situation with a trusted colleague or mentor for an outside perspective and advice.

CLOSING THOUGHTS:

This journaling has helped me see a pattern in my reactions to work situations. Recognizing my triggers is the first step towards managing my responses more effectively. I'm hopeful that with practice, I can improve my emotional self-regulation in similar situations."

IMPLEMENTING MINDFULNESS PRACTICES

Mindfulness is the practice of being fully present and engaged in the current moment. Incorporating mindfulness techniques, such as deep breathing exercises, meditation, or yoga, can help calm the mind and reduce the intensity of emotional reactions. These practices encourage a state of awareness that is conducive to thoughtful decision-making and emotional self-control.

Developing Cognitive Flexibility

Cognitive flexibility is the mental ability to switch between thinking about two different concepts or to think about multiple concepts simultaneously. Enhancing cognitive flexibility allows you to adapt your thought processes and behavior in the face of new, unexpected, or challenging circumstances. Techniques such as reframing thoughts, problem-solving exercises, and engaging in creative activities can improve this skill.

PRACTICING RESPONSE DELAY

The ability to delay responses to emotional triggers is a hallmark of self-regulation. This can be practiced by taking a moment to pause before reacting, allowing time for the initial emotional wave to pass and rational thought to emerge. Simple strategies include counting to ten, taking a few deep breaths, or removing yourself from a stressful situation if possible.

BUILDING RESILIENCE THROUGH EXPOSURE

Gradually exposing yourself to stressful situations can increase your tolerance and improve your ability to regulate emotions. Start with situations that are only mildly stressful, and work your way up to more challenging scenarios. By facing these situations head-on, you develop confidence in your ability to cope, which is essential for self-regulation.

REINFORCING POSITIVE BEHAVIOR

Positive reinforcement is a powerful tool for enhancing self-regulation. Reward yourself for successfully managing difficult emotions or for handling a challenging situation well. These rewards can be as simple as a favorite activity, a small treat, or positive self-talk. Over time, this reinforcement encourages a pattern of positive emotional control.

In summary, enhancing self-regulation is about understanding your emotional triggers, employing strategies to maintain control, and reinforcing positive behaviors. By cultivating these skills, you prepare yourself to face life's challenges with grace and determination, paving the way for success in all areas of your life.

FOSTERING MOTIVATION

Fostering motivation is an art that involves kindling the internal flames of passion, purpose, and persistence. This chapter will navigate you through actionable strategies to cultivate a robust and resilient motivation, crucial for achieving personal fulfillment and professional excellence.

IDENTIFYING PERSONAL DRIVERS

Begin by identifying what intrinsically motivates you. Is it the pursuit of knowledge, the satisfaction of completing tasks, or the joy of creative expression? Reflect upon moments when you felt most engaged and fulfilled to discern your natural inclinations and interests.

SETTING MEANINGFUL GOALS

Craft goals that resonate with your core values and aspirations. Use the SMART criteria to ensure they are Specific, Measurable, Achievable, Relevant, and Time-bound. Aligning your objectives with your inner drivers will provide a sense of purpose and direction.

CREATING A VISION BOARD

A vision board is a visual representation of your goals and dreams. It serves as a daily reminder of what you're striving towards. Populate your vision board with images, quotes, and symbols that represent your desired future and place it where you can see it regularly.

ESTABLISHING A ROUTINE

Build a routine that incorporates activities related to your goals. Consistency is key to maintaining motivation. Whether it's a daily reading habit, a workout schedule, or dedicated time for learning a new skill, a structured routine can help cement your commitment.

CULTIVATING OPTIMISM

Optimism fuels motivation. Practice reframing negative thoughts into positive ones. Acknowledge setbacks as opportunities for growth. Celebrate small victories along the way to maintain a positive outlook and keep the motivational momentum going.

FINDING A MENTOR OR ROLE MODEL

Connect with a mentor or choose a role model who embodies the success you aspire to. Their journey can provide inspiration, valuable insights, and a clear path to emulate. Their encouragement can also be a powerful motivator during challenging times.

HARNESSING THE POWER OF AFFIRMATIONS

Affirmations are positive statements that can help overcome self-sabotaging thoughts. Recite affirmations that reinforce your abilities and resolve.

For example, "I am capable of achieving my goals through dedication and effort."

TRACKING PROGRESS AND REFLECTING

Keep a log of your progress. Reflect on what you've learned, the obstacles you've overcome, and how you've grown. Regular reflection can bolster your motivation by providing concrete evidence of your advancements.

SURROUNDING YOURSELF WITH POSITIVITY

The company you keep can significantly influence your motivation. Surround yourself with positive, supportive people who believe in your goals and encourage your progress. Engage in communities that share your passions and ambitions.

CELEBRATING MILESTONES

Recognize and celebrate milestones, no matter how small. Acknowledging the steps you've completed towards your goals reinforces your motivation and provides the zest to continue your journey.

LEARNING CONTINUOUSLY

Adopt a mindset of lifelong learning. Stay curious and seek to learn something new every day. This not only broadens your horizons but also keeps your motivation fresh and dynamic.

In essence, fostering motivation is about connecting with your deepest desires and harnessing the daily habits that lead to success. By integrating the practical strategies laid out in this chapter into your life, you will create a self-sustaining cycle of motivation that propels you toward achieving your most ambitious goals.

CHAPTER 4
MASTER NEGATIVE EMOTIONS

In the intricate tapestry of human experience, negative emotions are as common as the threads of more joyful colors. Yet, unlike the hues that brighten our days, these darker strands can ensnare us, constricting our potential and clouding our path forward. Chapter 4 delves into the delicate art of mastering negative emotions, guiding you through the shadowy corridors of anxiety, stress, fear, and emotional exhaustion towards a place of greater calm and control.

Within these pages, we will explore the nuanced strategies designed to untangle the knots of anxiety, a feeling that can quicken the pulse and narrow our focus until little else seems to matter. We will then journey through the techniques to dismantle stress, that relentless pressure that can both motivate and overwhelm. Our exploration will take us through the shadows of fear, learning to understand its origins and how it can be transformed from a paralyzing force into a catalyst for growth.

As we venture further, we will confront the specter of emotional drain, that depletion of energy that can leave us feeling empty and detached. Through a series of insightful synthons, or synthesized insights, we will discover how to replenish our emotional reserves, restore our balance, and refine our resilience.

This chapter is not merely about negating negative emotions but about understanding and transforming them. It is about mastering the art of emotional alchemy, turning the base metals of our fears, anxieties, and stresses into the gold of insight, empowerment, and emotional intelligence. Join me on this journey to discover the strength that lies in the heart of vulnerability, and the power that awaits in the calm beyond the storm.

EMOTIONAL DRAIN

Emotional drain can leave us feeling exhausted and depleted, unable to meet the demands of daily life. Here are practical strategies and exercises designed to recharge your emotional batteries and address the core synthons of emotional drain.

Synthons of Emotional Drain and One - shot quick Tips (most of them are going to be analyzed better in the following sections):

1. Constant Fatigue Synthon:
- Strategy: Prioritize sleep and rest.
- Exercise: Develop a soothing bedtime routine to improve sleep quality.

2. Overwhelm Synthon:
- Strategy: Break down tasks into manageable steps.
- Exercise: Create a 'brain dump' list to get everything on paper and then organize it into a to-do list.

3. Irritability Synthon:
- Strategy: Identify triggers and develop coping mechanisms.
- Exercise: Practice deep-breathing or meditation when irritation begins to surface.

4. Lack of Joy Synthon:
- Strategy: Reengage with activities that bring happiness.
- Exercise: Schedule at least one enjoyable activity into your week, no matter how small.

5. Detachment Synthon:
- Strategy: Foster connections with others to counteract isolation.
- Exercise: Reach out to a friend or loved one for a chat or meet-up once a week.

6. Cognitive Fog Synthon:
- Strategy: Enhance mental clarity through diet and exercise.
- Exercise: Engage in a physical activity that also requires mental engagement, like dance or team sports.

7. *Anxiety Synthon:*

- Strategy: Develop anxiety-reducing techniques.
- Exercise: Practice guided imagery, envisioning a place where you feel calm and safe.

8. *Pessimism Synthon:*

- Strategy: Cultivate a positive mindset.
- Exercise: Challenge negative thoughts with evidence and reframe them in a positive light.

GENERAL PRACTICAL STRATEGIES:

1. *Scheduled Downtime:*

- Objective: To ensure regular intervals of rest and recovery.
- How-To: Block out periods in your schedule dedicated to relaxation or hobbies that rejuvenate you.

2. *Emotional Budgeting:*

- Objective: To allocate your emotional energy wisely throughout the day.
- How-To: List daily activities and assign an emotional 'cost' to each. Prioritize tasks that are fulfilling or essential and minimize those that drain you.

3. *Mindfulness Breaks:*

- Objective: To create pauses that refresh your mental state.
- How-To: Set a timer for every hour to take a few minutes to breathe deeply, stretch, or walk around.

EXERCISES FOR EMOTIONAL REPLENISHMENT:

1. The 4 A's Technique:
- Objective: To identify and manage emotional drain.
- How-To: Remember the 4 A's: Avoid unnecessary stress, Alter the situation, Adapt to stressors, and Accept what you can't change.

2. Five Senses Exercise:
- Objective: To ground yourself in the present and reduce stress.
- How-To: Take a moment to name five things you can see, four things you can touch, three things you can hear, two things you can smell, and one thing you can taste.

3. Gratitude Journaling:
- Objective: To shift focus from stress to appreciation.
- How-To: Write down three things you are grateful for each day, and reflect on why they bring you joy.

4. Breathing Techniques
- Objective: One of the most immediate ways to dampen the acute effects of anxiety is through controlled breathing.
- How-To: The 4-7-8 technique, for instance, requires you to inhale for 4 seconds, hold the breath for 7 seconds, and exhale slowly for 8 seconds. This helps regulate the nervous system and signals the body to relax.

By integrating these strategies and exercises into your routine, you can effectively combat emotional drain. Remember that consistent practice is key to making these techniques a natural part of your emotional toolkit.

THE ART OF MASTERING ANXIETY

Anxiety, a common human experience, can act as both a harbinger of caution and an impediment to action. Understanding and mastering it requires a blend of self-awareness, practical strategies, and a commitment to personal growth. This section of the chapter will focus on practical strategies for reducing the grip of anxiety on our lives.

UNDERSTANDING ANXIETY: THE THREEFOLD PATH

Anxiety, a common yet complex emotion, affects us on multiple levels: physical, mental, and spiritual. Recognizing and addressing anxiety across these dimensions can lead to a deeper understanding and more effective management of this challenging emotion.

THE PHYSICAL REALM: RECONNECTING WITH THE BODY

Often in the grip of anxiety, we lose touch with our physical selves. Our focus narrows to the tumultuous thoughts and fears swirling in our minds, leaving our body's signals unnoticed. The first step in mastering anxiety is to reconnect with and attend to these physical cues.

- Sensing the Signs: Anxiety manifests in various physical symptoms - tightness in the stomach, a constricted chest, or a lump in the throat. Becoming aware of these early signs is crucial. Instead of allowing them to amplify your anxiety, observe them with detachment.
- Breathing as a Tool: The breath is a powerful resource. By altering our breathing pattern - slowing and deepening it - we can activate the body's relaxation response. This physiological change sends a signal to the brain, indicating safety and calmness, thereby countering the body's anxious responses.

THE MENTAL DIMENSION: REFRAMING THOUGHTS

Our thoughts play a pivotal role in perpetuating anxiety. The narratives we construct and the meanings we assign to events can escalate or alleviate anxious feelings.

- Controlling the Narrative: Anxiety often stems from a desire to control the uncontrollable or a fear of the unpredictable. By consciously reframing our perspective, we can shift our focus from anxiety-inducing thoughts to those that promote peace and acceptance.
- The Power of Meditation: Meditation offers a structured way to strengthen our control over thoughts. It involves repeatedly redirecting our focus from distracting thoughts to a chosen point of concentration. This practice enhances our ability to guide our minds away from anxiety and towards positivity.
- Facing Fears: Confronting what we fear, rather than avoiding it, can significantly reduce anxiety's grip. Gradual exposure to the source of fear, in a controlled and safe environment, can lead to desensitization and empowerment.

THE SPIRITUAL ASPECT: FINDING SERENITY

The spiritual dimension offers perhaps the most profound resource for mastering anxiety. It involves understanding and accepting what we cannot change, finding courage to change what we can, and developing the wisdom to distinguish between the two.

- The Serenity Prayer: This prayer encapsulates the essence of spiritual mastery over anxiety. It guides us to accept our limitations while encouraging us to exert influence where possible, striking a balance between acceptance and action.
- Surrender and Trust: Spiritual practices, particularly those focused on surrender and trust, can be transformative. By cultivating a relation-

ship with a higher power or the universe, we gain a sense of being guided and supported, which can diminish feelings of anxiety.

- Meditation for Spiritual Growth: Regular meditation practice can deepen our connection to a source of infinite peace and love. This connection instills a profound sense of security, reducing fear and anxiety.

PERSONAL ANXIETY PLAN & SYSTEMATIC DESENSITIZATION

Gradually expose yourself to the source of your anxiety in controlled increments. This behavior therapy aims to reduce anxiety by encouraging a new response to the triggers. Create a personal anxiety management plan that includes identifying triggers, writing down coping strategies, and setting small, achievable goals. Keep a journal to document progress and reflect on what works for you. Engage in activities that reduce stress, such as yoga, art, or music. These can be particularly effective when combined with social interaction.

PRACTICAL STEPS TO MASTER ANXIETY

1. Physical Relaxation Techniques:
   - Practice deep, diaphragmatic breathing to activate the relaxation response.
   - Engage in physical activities or yoga to release tension.
   - Use mindfulness to become aware of physical sensations related to anxiety.
2. Mental Strategies:
   - Identify and challenge anxiety-inducing thoughts.
   - Use positive affirmations to reframe negative patterns.
   - Gradually expose yourself to feared situations in a controlled manner.
3. Spiritual Practices:

- Engage in daily meditation focusing on peace, love, or a higher power.
- Practice surrendering control and accepting what cannot be changed.
- Cultivate a sense of connectedness with a larger, benevolent universe.

A JOURNEY OF MASTERY

Mastering anxiety is not a destination but a journey, one that involves attention and practice across physical, mental, and spiritual realms. By embracing this holistic approach, we can navigate through anxiety with greater ease and resilience. Whether it's through conscious breathing, reframing our thoughts, or deepening our spiritual connections, each step we take is a stride towards a more serene and empowered life.

STRATEGIES TO ELIMINATE STRESS

In the labyrinth of stress management, exercise is often hailed as a panacea. However, its role is more intricate than a straightforward remedy. This chapter delves into the nuanced relationship between exercise and stress, unraveling the complexities and offering a balanced perspective for effective stress management.

PERSONAL EXERCISE PREFERENCES AND THEIR IMPACT

Individual preferences in exercise significantly influence its effect on stress. Some find solace in the rhythmic cadence of a run, where the release of endorphins brings calmness, countering the muscle tension typically associated with anxiety. Conversely, weight training might increase stress for others, as it imposes additional strain on an already tense body.

UNDERSTANDING THE SCIENCE

The scientific community acknowledges diverse impacts of different exercise forms on stress. Aerobic exercises, known for enhancing mood and alleviating stress, often overshadow the benefits of weight training in this context. However, individual experiences with these exercise forms can vary, underlining the importance of personalizing stress management strategies. Furthermore, a well-balanced diet supports a healthy body and mind. Consuming a variety of nutrients can boost your energy and immune system, helping to combat stress.

INTERVAL TRAINING: A NEUROLOGICAL APPROACH

Interval training, alternating between intense exertion and relaxation, presents an intriguing method of training the nervous system. This approach can potentially teach the body to transition swiftly from high-energy states to relaxation, offering a tool for better stress management.

EXERCISE: A STRESSOR ITSELF?

Contrary to popular belief, exercise doesn't always mitigate stress. It might offer a temporary escape, a brief respite through endorphin release, but it doesn't necessarily solve underlying stressors, such as financial worries. Recognizing this limitation is crucial in forming a holistic approach to stress management.

CHRONIC STRESS AND EXERCISE STRATEGY

Continuous stress necessitates a thoughtful approach to exercise. Rather than defaulting to high-intensity workouts, which might exacerbate stress, incorporating calming physical activities like yoga or a gentle jog can prove more beneficial in managing ongoing stress.

REFRAMING STRESS: A PHILOSOPHICAL PERSPECTIVE

How one perceives stress fundamentally alters its impact. Adopting a stoic mindset, focusing on elements within one's control, can significantly reduce stress. Viewing stress as a challenge or a byproduct of a meaningful life can transform one's reaction to stressful situations.

GOAL SETTING AND ITS STRESS IMPLICATIONS

Unrealistic goal setting can be a source of significant stress. Shifting focus from outcome to process, and setting achievable, flexible goals, can prevent the anxiety that comes with failing to meet overly ambitious targets.

CHANNELING STRESS THROUGH EXERCISE

For those who experience anxiety as an excess of energy, redirecting this energy into physical activity like brisk walking or high-intensity interval training can be an effective strategy. This approach aligns with the body's natural inclination to move under stress.

THE CRITICAL ROLE OF BREATHING TECHNIQUES

Breathing techniques are crucial in stress management. While deep diaphragmatic breathing induces relaxation, methods like the Wim Hof Technique, emphasizing rapid breathing, may not suit everyone, especially individuals with anxiety.

INCORPORATING RELAXATION PRACTICES

Daily practices like progressive muscle relaxation can prepare the body and mind for the day ahead, offering a buffer against stress. These techniques are particularly effective when stress levels are moderate.

A NEW PERSPECTIVE ON STRESS

Reframing stress, viewing it as an integral part of a life filled with purpose and challenges, can dramatically shift one's approach to stressful situations. This reframe encourages a more positive and proactive engagement with life's stressors.

TIME MANAGEMENT & ADOPT A POSITIVE MINDSET

Start by taking control of your tasks. Prioritize your duties and break them down into smaller, manageable parts. Use tools like planners and apps to keep track of deadlines and to-dos, which can provide a sense of control and accomplishment. Learn to say no, and delegate tasks when appropriate. Overcommitting can lead to burnout, while effective time management can help ensure you don't become overwhelmed. Reframe challenges as opportunities. Adopting a positive mindset can alter your perception of stressful situations, making them seem more manageable. Engage in activities you enjoy. Hobbies can divert your mind from stress and provide a sense of satisfaction and happiness. Ensure you get quality sleep. Sleep deprivation can significantly increase stress levels, while adequate rest can enhance your ability to deal with life's pressures.

SELF-REFLECTION & LIMIT EXPOSURE TO STRESSORS

Where possible, identify and reduce exposure to known stressors. This might mean setting boundaries in personal relationships or limiting time spent on social media.

Regularly spend time in self-reflection to understand the root causes of your stress. Journaling can help you track patterns and triggers, allowing for better management strategies.

Maintain a supportive network of friends and family. Socializing can provide a break from stress and offer solutions or distractions from life's pressures.

In conclusion, the role of exercise in managing stress is multifaceted and personal. A balanced approach, considering individual reactions, types of exercise, and broader perspectives on stress, is essential for effective stress management. This chapter underscores the importance of a personalized, holistic approach to exercise and stress, encouraging readers to find their unique path to stress resilience.

STRATEGIES TO ELIMINATE OUR FEAR

Fear is a primal human emotion that serves as a signal of potential danger, but it can often become a barrier to personal growth and happiness when it's out of proportion to actual risk. This section outlines strategies to tackle and reduce the grip of fear on our lives.

Fear can manifest in various aspects of life, hindering our ability to act and make decisions. To combat this, we can employ practical exercises that directly address and work to mitigate our fears.

FEAR MAPPING EXERCISE & 'WORST-CASE SCENARIO' ANALYSIS

- Objective: To identify specific fears and understand their triggers & to rationalize fear by understanding the worst outcomes.
- How-To: On a sheet of paper, write down a fear at the center. Draw branches that represent situations where this fear arises. Explore each situation, noting what triggers the fear and how you react. Focus on worst-case scenario of what you fear. Next, assess the likelihood of this happening and plan how you would cope or respond if it did occur. You can use the 'Three-Column' Technique' Draw three columns on a paper. In the first, write your fear-inducing thought. In the second, note the evidence that supports this thought. In the third, write evidence against it, and then formulate a more rational, balanced perspective.

PROGRESSIVE DESENSITIZATION

- Objective: To gradually reduce the fear response through controlled exposure.
- How-To: Create a hierarchy of fear-inducing situations from least to most frightening. Systematically expose yourself to these situations, starting from the bottom and working your way up, until the fear response diminishes.

ROLE-PLAYING

- Objective: To build confidence in handling fear-inducing interactions.
- How-To: With a friend or coach, role-play situations that you fear. This can help you practice and develop better coping mechanisms in a safe environment.

POWER POSES

- Objective: To use body language to reduce fear and increase confidence.
- How-To: Stand in a confident pose, such as with hands on hips and feet apart, for two minutes. This can help to decrease cortisol (stress hormone) levels and increase testosterone (confidence hormone) levels.

VISUALIZATION FOR SUCCESS

- Objective: To mentally rehearse successful outcomes.
- How-To: Close your eyes and vividly imagine a scenario where you face your fear and come out successful. Engage all your senses in this visualization.

SKILL-BUILDING ACTIVITIES

- Objective: To reduce fear by increasing competence.

- How-To: Identify skills that will help you overcome your fear and take courses or engage in self-teaching to improve these areas.

By regularly practicing these exercises, you can develop greater mastery over your fears. Over time, these strategies can enable you to approach fear-inducing situations with a stronger, more resilient mindset, diminishing the hold fear has on your life.

Incorporating these strategies into your daily life can help you manage, reduce, and even eliminate fears that hinder your personal and professional growth. This chapter aims to empower you with practical tools to confront and conquer your fears, fostering a life of courage and fulfillment.

THE ART OF EMOTIONAL INTELLIGENCE

CHAPTER 5

EMOTIONAL INTELLIGENCE IN RELATIONSHIPS

In the tapestry of human interactions, the threads of emotional intelligence (EQ) are interwoven throughout, creating patterns that can either be harmonious or discordant based on the skill of the weaver. The chapter that unfolds before you is a testament to the transformative power of

EQ within the realm of relationships - be they personal, professional, or parental.

We embark on this journey by cultivating empathy, the cornerstone of EQ, which transcends mere sympathy to form a bridge connecting our hearts to the experiences of others. This profound connection is more than an emotional response; it's a skill that, when mastered, allows us to understand deeply and respond to the silent cries and unspoken joy of those around us.

Understanding the types of empathy - cognitive, emotional, and compassionate - illuminates the multifaceted nature of this skill. Each type of empathy plays a unique role in how we relate to others and requires different approaches to develop fully. By exploring these variations, we enrich our EQ toolbox, enabling us to tailor our empathetic responses to the needs of each situation and individual.

The subsequent sections delve into enhancing communication and persuasion skills. We do not simply communicate to exchange information; we do so to connect, influence, and build trust. Similarly, persuasion is an art that, when infused with EQ, goes beyond convincing others to see our point of view - it becomes a mutual journey towards shared understanding and agreement.

Conflict is an inevitable guest in the house of relationships, but with enhanced conflict management skills, we learn to invite it in as a catalyst for growth rather than an adversary. Here, EQ serves as a mediator, guiding us to resolutions that honor all parties involved.

Our seven tips to live better relationships serve as practical steps towards embedding EQ into our daily interactions. Simple yet profound, these tips are the daily exercises for our emotional muscles.

Lastly, we turn to emotional intelligence in parenting, where EQ becomes the legacy we pass on to our children. It is in the nurturing environment of a home that the seeds of EQ are sown, promising a future generation more adept at navigating the complex emotional landscapes of their world.

This chapter offers a pathway to integrate EQ into the very essence of your daily existence, shifting it from abstract concept to active practice. Consider this not an exhaustive manual but a guiding compass, offering an overview and foundational principles to enhance your emotional fluency. By journeying through these pages, you embark on an exploration of emotional language, with the goal of nurturing and enriching the connections that form the fabric of your life. This chapter aims not to be the final word on EQ relationship management, but to provide you with the insights and guidelines that can illuminate the potential of every interaction you engage in.

CULTIVATING EMPATHY & TYPES OF EMPATHY

In the landscape of EQ, empathy stands as a central pillar, essential for building bridges between individuals, fostering understanding, and creating a nurturing environment. To cultivate empathy is to actively engage in the emotional experiences of others, to see the world through their eyes, and to feel the echoes of their joys and sorrows in our own hearts.

UNDERSTANDING THE TYPES OF EMPATHY

Empathy manifests in several forms, each serving a unique function in human connections:

Cognitive Empathy – This is the intellectual understanding of how someone else feels and thinks. It's empathy from a psychological perspective, allowing us to communicate more effectively because we can anticipate reactions and understand the motivations behind others' actions.

Emotional Empathy – This form goes deeper, involving a shared emotional response. It's the ability to physically feel what another person is experiencing, which can be both a powerful connector and, at times, overwhelming.

Compassionate Empathy – Beyond just understanding or feeling, compassionate empathy moves us to action. It compels us to help, whether through kind words, support, or more tangible aid.

PRACTICAL WAYS TO DEVELOP EMPATHY

Integrating empathy into your Emotional Quotient (EQ) is a dynamic process that requires consistent practice and application across various contexts. Developing empathy is not just about passive understanding; it requires active practice. Here are ways to cultivate each type of empathy:

COGNITIVE EMPATHY:

- Active Listening: Engage in conversations with the sole intent of understanding the other person's perspective. Practice listening without planning your response. Reflect on what is said and ask clarifying questions.
- Role-Playing: Imagine yourself in someone else's situation. This can be done through exercises where you adopt another person's role, whether in a simulated interaction or through journaling from their perspective.

Actionable methods and examples:

- Enhance this aspect by participating in forums or workshops that foster debate and discussion from multiple perspectives. For example, join a book club that reads and discusses literature from diverse cultures.

This exposes you to different viewpoints and challenges you to understand the narratives and emotions from the author's and characters' cultural contexts. Similarly, engage in workplace cross-functional team meetings where you can appreciate the different professional outlooks and how they shape each colleague's approach to problem-solving.

EMOTIONAL EMPATHY:

- Emotion Mapping: When interacting with others, take a moment to identify the emotions they might be feeling. Map these emotions onto your own experiences to find common emotional ground.
- Mindfulness Meditation: Engage in meditation focused on emotional awareness. Visualize connecting with others on an emotional level and practice feeling what they feel without judgment or an immediate need to resolve their issues.

Actionable methods and examples:

- To develop this, become part of support groups or online communities that focus on shared experiences. For instance, if you're interested in mental health, join a group that meets regularly to discuss personal journeys with anxiety or depression. Here, sharing your own feelings and actively listening to others can deepen your emotional understanding and connect you with the visceral aspects of their experiences.

COMPASSIONATE EMPATHY:

- Volunteering: Put your empathy into action by volunteering. Helping those in need can strengthen your compassionate response and make empathy a more automatic reaction.
- Kindness Practice: Challenge yourself to perform one unsolicited act of kindness each day. This could be as simple as offering a compli-

ment, giving up your seat on public transport, or helping a colleague with a task.

Actionable methods and examples:

- This is best practiced through action. Volunteer at a local shelter or food bank to connect with individuals from various walks of life. As you serve meals or provide support, you're not only recognizing the struggles of others but also actively contributing to their well-being. Additionally, participating in advocacy campaigns for social issues, like education reform or environmental protection, can fuel your drive to make a meaningful difference in response to the collective emotions and needs of a community.

By regularly engaging with activities that promote each type of empathy, you can enrich your EQ, leading to deeper connections and a more empathetic approach to both personal and professional relationships.

Remember, empathy is like a muscle - it strengthens with use. By practicing these exercises, you will not only become more attuned to the emotions of others but also develop a richer, more nuanced understanding of the complex tapestry of human experience. This understanding is vital for anyone seeking to enhance their EQ and, by extension, their personal and professional relationships.

ENHANCE COMMUNICATION SKILLS

Enhancing communication skills is pivotal in the domain of EQ, as it directly impacts one's ability to connect, understand, and be understood by others. This chapter will outline practical strategies to improve your communication capabilities, enabling you to express yourself clearly and effectively while also being receptive to the messages conveyed by those around you.

Conscious Listening: The cornerstone of EQ-driven communication is conscious listening. It goes beyond hearing words; it involves understanding the underlying emotions and intentions. Practice this by maintaining eye contact, nodding, and giving feedback such as, "What I hear you saying is…" This not only validates the speaker but also ensures you are truly grasping their message.

C.L. EXERCISE:

- Pair up with a partner and take turns being the speaker and listener.
- The speaker shares a recent experience while the listener practices active listening - this includes nodding, maintaining eye contact, and not interrupting.
- After speaking, the listener must summarize what they heard without adding personal opinions or advice.
- Swap roles and repeat the exercise.

Non-Verbal Cues: Your body language, facial expressions, and tone of voice convey much more than words alone. Develop an awareness of your non-verbal signals by recording yourself in conversations and observing your gestures and expressions. Are they congruent with your words? Aim to align your non-verbal communication with your verbal messages for coherence and clarity.

NON-VERBAL COMMUNICATION EXERCISE:

- Stand in front of a mirror and practice expressing different emotions with your face and body, without speaking.
- Record yourself having a conversation, then watch the playback focusing on your non-verbal cues. Take notes on what non-verbal messages you're sending.

- Ask for feedback from friends or family about your non-verbal communication and work on aligning it with your verbal messages.

Empathetic Responding: Utilize empathetic language that shows you are not just listening but also feeling with the speaker. Phrases like "That sounds really challenging," or "I can imagine how that must feel," demonstrate emotional solidarity and encourage further sharing.

EMPATHETIC LANGUAGE ROLE-PLAY:

- In pairs, role-play different scenarios that require empathy (e.g., consoling a friend who has lost a job).
- Practice using empathetic statements and observe the other person's reaction.
- Discuss after each role-play what felt genuine and what could be improved.

Clarity and Conciseness: EQ-infused communication is free from unnecessary jargon and complexity. Strive for simplicity and precision in your language. Before speaking, take a moment to organize your thoughts to ensure your message is understood as intended.

CLARITY IN COMMUNICATION PRACTICE:

- Choose a complex topic you are familiar with and explain it to someone who has no background knowledge in that area.
- Focus on using clear, concise language and avoid technical jargon.
- Ask for feedback on the clarity of your explanation and refine your approach based on the feedback.

Feedback: Learn to give and receive feedback in a manner that is constructive and empathetic. Use the "sandwich" method – start with a positive note, address the area for improvement, and end with encouragement. When receiving feedback, listen with an open mind, ask clarifying questions, and express gratitude for the opportunity to grow.

FEEDBACK EXERCISE:

- Write down recent feedback you've received and reflect on your initial emotional response.
- Practice responding to feedback constructively by drafting responses that express openness to growth.
- Role-play giving and receiving feedback with a peer, focusing on using the "sandwich" method.

Conflict Resolution: Effective communication is key when navigating disagreements. Approach conflicts with a mindset of finding a solution rather than winning an argument. Acknowledge the other person's perspective and work together to reach a mutually beneficial outcome.

CONFLICT RESOLUTION SCENARIO SIMULATION:

- Create a scenario involving a conflict situation.
- With a partner, practice resolving the conflict by each expressing your viewpoints and then working together to find a solution.
- Reflect on the communication strategies used and how they helped or hindered the resolution process.

By incorporating these EQ-centric communication strategies into your daily interactions, you will see a transformation in your relationships. Your conversations will become more engaging, your connections deeper, and your personal and professional rapport will be strengthened.

ENHANCE PERSUASION SKILLS

Enhancing persuasion skills in the context of Emotional Intelligence (EQ) involves far more than just the ability to argue convincingly. It's about understanding and connecting with people on an emotional level to influence their thoughts and actions. Persuasion, when aligned with EQ, transforms from mere manipulation to a skill that fosters positive relationships and outcomes.

UNDERSTANDING EQ IN PERSUASION

EMOTIONAL AWARENESS AND EMPATHY:

At the heart of EQ-based persuasion is emotional awareness and empathy. To persuade effectively, one must be adept at reading the emotional states of others, understanding their needs, desires, and fears. Empathy allows a person to see the world from another's perspective, making it easier to find common ground and address concerns that might be barriers to persuasion.

SELF-AWARENESS AND REGULATION:

Self-awareness in EQ helps in recognizing one's own emotional triggers and biases in persuasion. A high EQ persuader is aware of their own emotional state and can regulate emotions to remain calm and focused, even in the face of resistance or challenges.

EFFECTIVE COMMUNICATION:

EQ enhances communication skills, making it easier to convey messages in a way that resonates with others. It involves active listening, understanding non-verbal cues, and speaking in a way that is clear, respectful, and aligned with the listener's values and emotions.

STRATEGIES TO ENHANCE PERSUASION SKILLS THROUGH EQ

BUILDING RAPPORT:

Creating a connection with the person you are trying to persuade is crucial. Establish trust and rapport by showing genuine interest in their thoughts and feelings. Use open body language, maintain eye contact, and actively listen. People are more likely to be persuaded when they feel understood and respected.

TAILORING THE MESSAGE:

Different people respond to different types of persuasion. Some may be motivated by facts and logic, while others are moved by emotional appeals. High EQ allows for the flexibility to adapt the style of persuasion to suit the individual's preferences. This could mean using stories and anecdotes for some, while employing data and evidence for others.

EMOTIONAL APPEAL:

People are often more influenced by how they feel about something than just the facts. Use emotional appeals to create a compelling narrative around your argument. This doesn't mean manipulating emotions, but rather aligning your message with values and emotions that are important to the listener.

MANAGING RESISTANCE:

Resistance is a natural part of any persuasive effort. High EQ enables you to handle objections gracefully without getting defensive. Acknowledge the other person's concerns, show empathy, and provide reassurance or additional information to alleviate their apprehensions.

INFLUENCING THROUGH INSPIRATION:

Inspire others by painting a picture of what could be achieved. People are often persuaded when they see the higher purpose or the bigger picture. Use your EQ to align your persuasive efforts with the listener's aspirations and values.

PRACTICING PATIENCE AND PERSISTENCE:

Persuasion often requires patience. High EQ equips you with the emotional resilience to stay the course, even when immediate results aren't visible. Maintain a positive and optimistic outlook, as this can be infectious and more likely to sway others over time.

CONTINUOUS LEARNING AND ADAPTATION:

Finally, enhancing EQ-based persuasion skills is a continuous process. Reflect on your interactions, learn from successes and failures, and be open to adjusting your approach. Seek feedback and use it to refine your persuasion techniques.

In conclusion, integrating EQ into your persuasion skills means moving beyond mere rhetoric to building meaningful connections. It's about influencing others not just for immediate gain, but for mutual benefit and positive outcomes. With high EQ, persuasion becomes an art – one that fosters understanding, respect, and collaborative success.

ENHANCE CONFLICT MANAGEMENT SKILLS

Enhancing conflict management skills in conjunction with Emotional Intelligence (EQ) is essential for navigating disagreements constructively. Conflicts, whether in personal relationships or professional settings, are inevitable. However, handling them with a high degree of emotional intelligence can transform potential confrontations into opportunities for growth, understanding, and problem-solving.

THE ROLE OF EQ IN CONFLICT MANAGEMENT

UNDERSTANDING AND MANAGING EMOTIONS:

Central to EQ is the ability to understand and manage one's own emotions, as well as recognize and respond appropriately to the emotions of others. In conflict situations, emotions can run high, and the ability to remain calm and composed is crucial. A person with high EQ can identify and regulate their emotional responses, preventing escalation and maintaining a focus on resolution.

EMPATHY:

Empathy is a cornerstone of EQ and plays a vital role in conflict management. It involves understanding the perspectives and feelings of others, even if one does not agree with them. Empathetic listening can de-escalate tension and create a space where all parties feel heard and understood, paving the way for collaborative solutions.

EFFECTIVE COMMUNICATION:

EQ enhances communication skills, making it easier to articulate thoughts and feelings clearly and respectfully during conflicts. This includes the ability to express oneself assertively without being aggressive, and to listen actively to others' viewpoints.

STRATEGIES TO ENHANCE CONFLICT MANAGEMENT SKILLS THROUGH EQ

SELF-REFLECTION AND EMOTIONAL AWARENESS:

Before addressing the conflict, take time to reflect on your own feelings and the root causes of the disagreement. Understanding your emotional triggers helps in approaching the conflict with clarity and composure. Practice active listening, which involves fully concentrating on what is being said rather than just passively 'hearing' the message of the speaker. Reflect back what you have heard and ask clarifying questions. This demonstrates respect for the other person's perspective and helps to clarify misunderstandings.

CREATING A SAFE ENVIRONMENT FOR DIALOGUE:

Start the conversation by establishing mutual respect and a willingness to understand each other. Assure all parties that their viewpoints are valuable. This sets a tone of cooperation rather than confrontation.

ACKNOWLEDGING AND VALIDATING EMOTIONS:

Recognize and validate the emotions of all parties involved, even if you disagree with their stance. Acknowledgment can defuse hostility and shows empathy.

UTILIZING NON-CONFRONTATIONAL LANGUAGE:

Use "I" statements instead of "You" statements to express your feelings and needs. For example, say "I feel frustrated when…" instead of "You always make me feel…". This reduces defensiveness and focuses on your experience rather than placing blame.

SEEKING COMMON GROUND:

Look for areas of agreement that can serve as a foundation for resolving the conflict. Focusing on common goals and shared values can shift the conversation from adversarial to cooperative.

BRAINSTORMING SOLUTIONS TOGETHER:

Engage all parties in brainstorming potential solutions. This collaborative approach not only leads to more creative solutions but also ensures buy-in from everyone involved.

MANAGING STRESS AND EMOTIONS:

During the conflict, if emotions begin to escalate, take a break to cool down. Managing your stress levels is key to maintaining clear thinking and effective communication.

LEARNING FROM CONFLICT:

View conflicts as learning opportunities. Reflect on what worked well and what could be improved. This continuous learning approach can enhance your EQ and conflict management skills over time.

SEEKING HELP WHEN NEEDED:

Recognize when it's necessary to involve a neutral third party, such as a mediator, to help resolve the conflict. There's strength in acknowledging when situations are beyond your current skill set.

In conclusion, integrating EQ into conflict management involves a combination of self-awareness, empathy, effective communication, and a collaborative approach. By viewing conflicts as opportunities for growth and understanding, and by applying EQ principles, you can navigate even the most challenging situations more effectively, leading to healthier relationships and more productive outcomes.

7 + 1 TIPS TO LIVE BETTER A RELATIONSHIP

Building a healthy relationship requires effort, commitment, and the willingness to evolve with your partner. Whether it's a blossoming connection or a long-term partnership, the path to a fulfilling relationship involves several key steps and principles.

FOUNDATION OF A HEALTHY RELATIONSHIP

Healthy relationships share certain characteristics, including a deep emotional connection, common goals, and mutual respect. Feeling loved is distinct from being loved - it's about feeling understood and valued. Communication is paramount; partners must feel safe to express concerns and resolve conflicts without fear or degradation.

MAINTAINING CONNECTION AND INTEREST

A relationship thrives on involvement and emotional connection. This means not shying away from disagreements and ensuring that both partners maintain their own identities, hobbies, and social circles. Stagnation often occurs when couples stop engaging with each other emotionally and fail to maintain the interests and external relationships that enrich their lives.

COMMUNICATION AND UNDERSTANDING

Open, honest communication is the bedrock of a healthy relationship. It's essential to express needs and desires clearly, as assumptions can lead to misunderstandings. Understanding your partner's nonverbal cues is as crucial as verbal communication. This requires attentive listening and a willingness to engage with your partner's emotional state.

PHYSICAL INTIMACY AND SHARED EXPERIENCES

Physical contact and shared experiences foster closeness. This doesn't solely refer to sexual intimacy but also to simple gestures like holding hands or hugging. Trying new activities together can introduce excitement, and working on projects that benefit others can strengthen your bond.

BALANCE AND COMPROMISE

Healthy relationships involve give and take. Recognizing and valuing what's important to your partner, and vice versa, is key to a balanced relationship. Compromise doesn't mean one always acquiesces to the other; instead, it's about finding a middle ground where both partners feel their needs are met.

CONFLICT RESOLUTION

Disagreements are natural, but how they're handled is what counts. Fair fighting, forgiveness, and a willingness to resolve conflicts constructively are vital. Letting go of grudges and focusing on the present helps prevent lingering resentments.

NAVIGATING CHALLENGES

Recognize that relationships face ups and downs. Stressful external factors, like job loss or health issues, can strain a relationship. Coping with these together, with patience and understanding, rather than taking stress out on each other, can strengthen your connection.

SUSTAINING LOVE

Keeping the spark of love alive requires conscious effort. Reminiscing about the beginning of your relationship, being open to change, and seeking external support when needed can help maintain the bond.

Ultimately, healthy relationships are about growth, understanding, and a shared journey. It involves continuous learning and adapting, not only as individuals but as partners in a dynamic, loving relationship.

EMOTIONAL INTELLIGENCE IN PARENTING

Emotional intelligence (EQ) is an invaluable tool in the delicate art of parenting. It encompasses the ability to understand and manage one's own emotions, as well as the capacity to empathize with and influence the feelings of others – in this case, our children. This chapter explores the role of EQ in fostering nurturing relationships between parents and their children, aiming to cultivate a home environment that promotes mutual respect, understanding, and emotional growth.

THE IMPORTANCE OF MODELING EMOTIONAL INTELLIGENCE

Children learn emotional regulation and understanding largely through observation and imitation. Parents who exhibit high EQ provide a model for their children to emulate. For instance, a parent who can remain calm and articulate during moments of stress teaches their child to do the same. When a child witnesses their parent handling disappointment with grace, they learn resilience. Conversely, a parent who reacts to frustration with outbursts or withdrawal may inadvertently teach their child to respond to their emotions in kind.

EMPATHY: THE HEART OF CONNECTION

Empathy is the cornerstone of an emotionally intelligent parenting approach. It involves more than simply understanding a child's emotions; it requires parents to put themselves in their child's shoes and offer genuine compassion. When a child is upset, an empathetic response might be, "It sounds like you're really hurt by what happened. I understand why that would upset you." This kind of response validates the child's feelings and can help them process their emotions in a healthy way.

OPEN COMMUNICATION: A TWO-WAY STREET

Establishing open lines of communication is essential. Encourage children to express their feelings by asking open-ended questions and listening actively. Avoid dismissing or minimizing their emotions, which can lead to feelings of isolation or misunderstanding. Instead, help them to name their emotions and discuss them openly. This practice not only strengthens the parent-child bond but also equips children with the language they need to articulate their feelings.

SELF-REGULATION: LEADING BY EXAMPLE

Self-regulation is another key aspect of EQ in parenting. Parents must be aware of their own emotional triggers and learn to manage their responses. If a parent becomes easily angered by a child's questioning or challenging behavior, it's crucial to understand the root of this frustration and address it constructively. Demonstrating self-regulation in the face of challenges teaches children to do the same.

DISCIPLINE AND EQ: GUIDANCE OVER PUNISHMENT

Discipline through an EQ lens focuses on teaching rather than punishing. It means setting clear boundaries and consequences but doing so with empathy and an eye towards teaching better behavior. It's about helping children understand the impact of their actions and guiding them to make amends and learn from their mistakes.

EMOTIONAL COACHING: GUIDING EMOTIONAL GROWTH

Emotional coaching involves guiding children through their emotional experiences. When a child is struggling, instead of offering immediate solutions or dismissing the problem, a parent can help them work through their emotions. This process includes acknowledging the emotion, helping the child understand it, and exploring constructive ways to address the situation.

THE LONG-TERM IMPACT OF EQ IN PARENTING

When parents integrate EQ into their parenting, they help foster emotionally healthy children who are better equipped to face the challenges of life. These children are more likely to develop strong interpersonal skills, empathy, and resilience. They are also more apt to perform well academically and maintain better mental health.

In conclusion, EQ is not just an asset for parents; it's a gift to their children. By prioritizing emotional intelligence in the parent-child relationship, parents sow seeds of emotional wellness that can grow throughout their children's lives, leading to more fulfilling relationships and better overall well-being.

CHAPTER 6

EMOTIONAL INTELLIGENCE AT WORK

In the dynamic and often challenging environment of the workplace, the role of emotional intelligence (EQ) becomes not just beneficial, but essential. This chapter delves into the multifaceted application of EQ within professional settings. Our journey through this chapter will explore how emotional intelligence can transform our work experience, enhance team dynamics, and foster leadership and personal growth.

At the core of this exploration lies the understanding that EQ is more than just a personal attribute; it's a critical professional skill. We'll investigate how self-awareness, empathy, effective communication, and emotional regulation can significantly impact decision-making, conflict resolution, and team collaboration. The chapter will also provide practical insights on how to navigate workplace challenges using EQ, turning potential obstacles into opportunities for professional development and success.

Whether you're a team member, a leader, or an entrepreneur, understanding and applying the principles of emotional intelligence at work can lead to more fulfilling and productive professional relationships and outcomes. From dealing with stress and managing change to inspiring and leading others, EQ is an invaluable tool in the modern professional's toolkit.

As we progress, we'll uncover real-world examples, strategies, and exercises designed to enhance your emotional intelligence skills in the workplace. This chapter aims not only to enlighten you about the importance of EQ at work but also to equip you with the tools and knowledge to actively integrate and leverage these skills in your daily professional life

WHY IS SO IMPORTANT TO HAVE EQ EMPLOYEES?

In the contemporary business landscape, the significance of Emotional Intelligence (EQ) in employees has surged to the forefront, particularly concerning their ability to make informed and effective decisions. This chapter explores why emotionally intelligent employees are indispensable assets when it comes to decision-making processes within an organization.

Firstly, EQ imbues employees with the capacity to manage their own emotions and understand the emotions of others, allowing for clearer thought processes and less bias in decision-making. Emotionally intelligent employees are adept at navigating through their feelings without letting transient emotions cloud their judgement. For instance, an employee with high EQ is less likely to make a hasty business decision out of frustration or stress, instead, they evaluate the situation with a level head, considering the long-term effects of their choices.

Moreover, such employees are generally more empathetic, which translates into better understanding the needs and perspectives of colleagues, clients, and stakeholders. This empathy enables them to factor in a wider range of perspectives, leading to more inclusive and well-rounded decisions. They can anticipate the emotional impact of decisions on others, thereby foreseeing potential issues and addressing them proactively.

The self-awareness component of EQ also ensures that employees are cognizant of their own strengths and limitations. They can objectively assess a situation, recognize when they need additional input or expertise, and are not averse to seeking help or advice. This openness to learning and collaboration not only improves the quality of decisions made but also fosters a culture of shared knowledge and continuous improvement.

Emotionally intelligent employees also exhibit superior conflict resolution skills. In decision-making, conflicts are inevitable, but EQ-equipped individuals can navigate these conflicts constructively. They bring people together, bridge divides, and find solutions that serve the broader objectives of the organization rather than individual agendas.

Another aspect where EQ plays a pivotal role is adaptability. The business environment is in constant flux, and decisions must often be made with incomplete information or under pressure. Employees with high EQ are more adaptable and resilient; they remain calm under pressure and are able to adjust their decision-making approach as new information becomes available.

Furthermore, emotionally intelligent employees tend to be more motivated by internal drivers such as personal growth and a desire to contribute positively to their organization, rather than external rewards. This intrinsic motivation leads to decisions that are more aligned with the company's values and long-term goals.

In summary, EQ is not just a nice-to-have quality in employees; it is a critical component that underpins effective decision-making. As organizations navigate complex challenges and opportunities, EQ empowers employees to make decisions that are thoughtful, inclusive, balanced, and ultimately, drive the organization forward. By valuing and developing emotional intelligence within their workforce, companies can ensure that their decision-makers are equipped to lead with wisdom and insight, heralding a future of sustained success and adaptability in an ever-changing world.

BETTER DECISION MAKERS

In the realm of business, EQ shapes individuals into better decision-makers, transforming the organizational canvas with strokes of insight, empathy, and strategic foresight.

Emotionally intelligent decision-makers possess an acute self-awareness that allows them to recognize their emotional states and biases, thereby preventing these from skewing their judgement. They can detach from the heat of the moment, stepping back to appraise the situation with clarity and objectivity. This self-regulation is essential when decisions must be made under pressure, ensuring choices are based on fact rather than feeling.

Morcover, their ability to empathize plays a crucial role. They see through the lenses of diverse stakeholders, understanding the ripples their decisions will create across the ecosystem of the workplace. This comprehensive perspective fosters decisions that are not only smart but also socially sensitive, balancing business acumen with human understanding.

EQ also enhances communication, a cornerstone of collaborative decision-making. Emotionally intelligent individuals are adept at articulating their thought processes and reasoning, inviting constructive dialogue and building consensus. They listen as much as they lead, integrating feedback and insights into well-rounded, collective decisions.

In essence, decision-makers with high EQ lead not with impulse but with informed intuition, not with rigidity but with resilience. They are the architects of a future where the wisdom of the mind is in harmony with the intelligence of the heart, crafting decisions that stand the test of time and tide. The result is a workforce that navigates the complexities of the corporate world with agility, creativity, and a profound understanding of the human element at the heart of every business venture.

EXERCISE: DECISION-MAKING REFLECTION

Objective: Enhance emotional intelligence in decision-making at work.

Duration: Weekly, 15-20 minutes.

How-to:

- **Identify a Recent Decision:** At the end of each week, select a significant decision you made in the workplace.
- **Analyze Your Emotional State:** Reflect on the emotions you experienced during the decision-making process. Were you stressed,

anxious, confident, or excited? Acknowledge these emotions without judgment.

- **Evaluate Biases and Triggers:** Consider any personal biases or emotional triggers that may have influenced your decision. Did past experiences or personal preferences play a role? Be honest in your assessment.

- **Consider Stakeholder Perspectives:** Think about the decision from the viewpoint of different stakeholders (employees, colleagues, clients). How might your decision impact them? This step enhances empathy and broadens your perspective.

- **Assess Communication:** Reflect on how you communicated the decision. Did you listen to others' opinions and integrate their feedback? How effective was your communication in building consensus or understanding?

- **Outcome Analysis:** Evaluate the decision's outcome. Did it align with your professional values and objectives? What could have been done differently?

- **Personal Growth Plan:** Based on your reflection, identify areas for growth. Set goals for improving emotional awareness, empathy, or communication in future decision-making scenarios.

- **Journaling:** Document your reflections and insights in a journal to track your growth in emotional intelligence over time.

This exercise aims to cultivate self-awareness, empathy, and effective communication in decision-making, key components of emotional intelligence in the workplace.

HANDLE PRESSURE

In the fast-paced work environment, handling pressure is an indispensable skill. It's about recognizing stressors, understanding their impact, and responding effectively. Mastering this skill is crucial for maintaining productivity, mental well-being, and fostering a positive workplace culture. As we explore techniques to handle pressure, we focus on developing a blend of self-awareness, motivation, empathy, and social skills, turning workplace challenges into opportunities for growth and success.

EXERCISE TO TRAIN HANDLING PRESSURE

Objective: Develop resilience to pressure in the workplace.

Duration: Daily, 10 minutes.

How-to:

* **Mindful Breathing:** Start each day with a five-minute mindful breathing session to ground yourself and prepare for potential stressors.
* **Recognize Stress Signals:** Throughout the day, periodically check in with yourself. Notice any signs of stress like tense muscles or rapid breathing.
* **Pressure Log:** Keep a small journal. Note down moments when you felt under pressure, describing the situation, your response, and the outcome.
* **Reflect and Plan:** End your day with a reflection on the stressors you faced. Identify what worked and what didn't in your response.
* **Seek Feedback:** Regularly discuss your handling of pressure with a mentor or colleague. Gain insights and alternative strategies.

This exercise encourages proactive management of stress, enhancing one's ability to handle pressure with poise and efficiency.

Example - Journal Entry: Pressure Log

Date: January 15, 2023

Critical Situation: High-Stakes Client Presentation

DESCRIPTION OF THE SITUATION:

Today, I faced a high-pressure situation at work. We had a crucial client presentation, and it was imperative to secure this deal for our company. As the lead on this project, the responsibility weighed heavily on me. The client had a reputation for being hard to please, and our team had been working tirelessly for weeks to prepare.

PHYSICAL AND EMOTIONAL RESPONSES:

* Physical Signs: As the presentation time approached, I noticed my heart rate increasing and my palms getting sweaty. My breathing became shallow, and I had a slight headache.
* Emotional Responses: I felt a mix of anxiety and determination. There was fear of failure, coupled with a strong desire to succeed.

REFLECTING ON THE SITUATION:

* Self-Awareness: Recognizing these physical signs of stress, I realized I needed to manage my response proactively.
* Self-Regulation: I took a few minutes to practice deep breathing and mindfulness to calm my nerves. I reminded myself of the preparation and hard work we had put in.
* Motivation: Focusing on the bigger picture and the positive impact this deal would have on our company helped to realign my thoughts.
* Empathy and Social Skills: I took a moment to acknowledge that my team might also be feeling similar pressures. We had a quick huddle,

where I shared some encouraging words and listened to any last-minute concerns.

OUTCOME:

The presentation went better than expected. Despite the initial nerves, once I started, I felt more in control. The client was impressed with our proposal, and we received positive feedback. This situation was a learning experience in managing pressure effectively.

Planning for Future High-Pressure Situations:

- Develop a Pre-Presentation Routine: Incorporate relaxation techniques like deep breathing or a short walk before future high-stakes meetings.
- Regular Team Check-Ins: Before critical events, check in with the team to encourage and support each other.
- Reflection Post-Event: Dedicate time after high-pressure situations to analyze what went well and areas for improvement.

This journal entry not only helped me process the day's events but also provided a blueprint for handling similar situations in the future.

BETTER ENVIRONMENT AT WORK

A nurturing work environment is the bedrock of productivity and innovation, and emotional intelligence (EQ) is its landscaper. When EQ principles are applied, they till the soil of the workplace, allowing a more congenial and collaborative atmosphere to take root.

Self-aware leaders set the tone by modeling emotional transparency and balance. Their self-regulation creates a calm and secure space for others to express ideas without fear of harsh judgment. This establishes a culture where feedback is not a weapon but a tool for growth.

The empathy component of EQ is like sunlight, vital for a healthy work environment. Leaders and employees who can understand and share the feelings of their colleagues create an emotionally safe space. This empathy fosters genuine connections and a sense of belonging among team members, which in turn leads to a supportive and unified workforce.

Social skills serve as the water, essential for the environment to flourish. Communication, conflict resolution, and collaboration are the channels through which the lifeblood of a positive workplace flows. Proficiency in these areas ensures that interactions are not just transactions but opportunities for mutual advancement and understanding.

In essence, leveraging EQ to enhance the workplace environment is about cultivating an ecosystem where everyone can thrive. It's about creating conditions where the organizational climate is conducive to growth, satisfaction, and collective success.

Creating a better work environment is a multifaceted task that requires thoughtful leadership. A leader can take several actions to foster a positive, productive, and inclusive workplace:

- **Open Communication:** Establish channels for open and transparent communication. Encourage team members to voice their opinions, concerns, and ideas. This can be through regular meetings, suggestion boxes, or open-door policies. Effective communication builds trust and makes employees feel valued and heard.

- **Recognition and Appreciation:** Regularly acknowledge and appreciate the efforts and achievements of team members. Recognition can be as simple as a verbal thank you, a written note, or more formal rewards and incentives. This appreciation boosts morale and motivates employees.

- **Professional Development:** Invest in the growth and development of employees. Offer training opportunities, workshops, and mentorship programs. When employees feel their career growth is supported, they are more engaged and committed.

- **Work-Life Balance:** Promote a healthy balance between work and personal life. Encourage taking breaks, offer flexible working hours or remote work options when possible. A focus on work-life balance reduces burnout and increases job satisfaction.

- **Foster Team Collaboration:** Create opportunities for team building and collaboration. This could be through collaborative projects, team meetings, or social events. A collaborative environment enhances team spirit and brings diverse perspectives and skills to the table.

- **Constructive Feedback:** Provide regular, constructive feedback in a manner that is encouraging and focused on growth. This helps employees understand their strengths and areas for improvement.

- **Inclusive Culture:** Promote diversity and inclusivity. Respect and value differences in opinions, backgrounds, and perspectives. An inclusive culture makes employees feel safe and respected, leading to a more creative and innovative workplace.

- **Conflict Resolution:** Address conflicts swiftly and fairly. Adopt a problem-solving approach that focuses on the issue, not the individuals involved. Efficient conflict management prevents negative emotions from festering and maintains a harmonious work environment.

- **Physical Environment:** Ensure that the physical workspace is comfortable, safe, and conducive to productivity. This can include ergonomic furniture, appropriate lighting, and recreational spaces.

- **Empowerment and Autonomy:** Empower employees by entrusting them with responsibilities and allowing them the autonomy to make decisions in their areas of work. This boosts confidence and fosters a sense of ownership and responsibility.

By taking these actions, a leader can significantly enhance the work environment, leading to increased employee satisfaction, higher productivity, and overall organizational success.

MOTIVATION

Motivation is often misconceived as a switch that can be flipped on or off in people, leading to the misguided notion that one can simply 'motivate the unmotivated'. Yet, true motivation is inherently more complex, woven intrinsically into the fabric of our emotional intelligence. It is not merely about dangling carrots or brandishing sticks to elicit the behaviors we desire. Such tactics may compel action, but they rarely kindle the fires of loyalty, love, or genuine commitment.

The key to understanding motivation lies not in coercion, but in inspiration. When people seem unmotivated, it is often not a flaw within them, but a mismatch between their inner drives and their external environment. They may feel out of place, unnoticed, or undervalued. Perhaps fear grips them, or they simply lack the necessary preparation. Emotional intelligence prompts us to look beyond the surface of 'unmotivation' and to consider a myriad of underlying factors.

An emotionally intelligent approach to motivation involves creating a culture where individuals feel seen, heard, and valued. It's about fostering an environment where the sense of belonging and significance prevails, where the vision and cause transcend the mundanity of tasks. In such a culture, motivation flourishes naturally because people are aligned with the work they do; they believe in its purpose, and they feel integral to the success of the whole.

The task of the leader, then, is not to motivate but to inspire - to connect individuals to a collective cause that resonates deeply with their own values and aspirations. This is where the components of emotional intelligence - self-awareness, self-regulation, empathy, and social skills - become pivotal. Leaders who embody these traits can identify the emotional currents flowing through their teams and navigate them towards a shared horizon.

Empathy allows leaders to understand what drives their team members, to recognize their aspirations and fears. With this insight, they can tailor opportunities and challenges that spark intrinsic motivation, kindling a passion for achievement that burns from within, rather than being imposed from without.

Self-awareness and self-regulation ensure that leaders model the very motivation they wish to see in others. They demonstrate commitment, resilience, and a positive outlook, showing how setbacks can be stepping stones to greater achievements. In doing so, they become beacons of inspiration that others are drawn to follow.

Finally, adept social skills enable leaders to communicate the vision compellingly, to foster collaboration and to build strong bonds within the team. They create an atmosphere where everyone contributes, and individual successes are celebrated as collective triumphs.

In this emotionally intelligent paradigm, motivation is not an external reward but an internal state that flourishes in the right conditions. It is sustained by a sense of purpose, by the joy of contributing to something meaningful, and by the satisfaction of personal growth. When these elements are in place, people don't just work for a paycheck; they work for the profound fulfillment that comes from knowing they are part of something greater than themselves.

Thus, the art of fostering motivation transcends the simplistic notions of reward and punishment. It is about cultivating an environment where people can connect their personal drives to a collective journey. It is about leading in a way that resonates with the core of human emotions, harnessing the power of emotional intelligence to create a force of motivated, inspired, and emotionally invested individuals.

To foster a better work environment and motivate employees, a company should focus on specific emotional intelligence-driven actions:

- **Regular Recognition:** Acknowledge individual efforts and achievements to make team members feel valued.
- **Open Communication:** Establish channels for employees to freely share ideas and feedback.
- **Aligning Goals:** Help employees connect their personal goals with the organization's objectives.
- **Safe and Inclusive Environment:** Create a workplace where all employees feel psychologically safe and respected.
- **Empowerment and Trust:** Delegate responsibilities and trust employees with autonomy over their tasks.
- **Exemplary Leadership:** Lead by example in demonstrating desired behaviors and attitudes.
- **Growth Opportunities:** Provide opportunities for professional development and skill acquisition.
- **Regular Personal Check-Ins:** Conduct one-on-one meetings to discuss each team member's progress and challenges.
- **Work-Life Balance:** Encourage a balance between professional responsibilities and personal time.
- **Empathetic Conflict Resolution:** Address conflicts with understanding, ensuring fair resolutions.

- **Sharing Successes and Learning from Failures:** Celebrate team achievements and view setbacks as learning experiences.

These strategies are aimed at enhancing motivation through recognition, communication, goal alignment, inclusivity, trust, personal growth, and balanced conflict resolution.

CHAPTER 7

CASE STUDIES

REAL-WORLD EXAMPLES OF EQ IN ACTION

The concept of Emotional Intelligence (EQ) resonates across a multitude of domains, signifying its fundamental importance. However, its abstract nature often necessitates a grounded understanding through real-world examples. This section ventures to elucidate the essence of EQ by exploring instances where Emotional Intelligence markedly influences outcomes in personal and professional spheres.

1. CONFLICT RESOLUTION:

In a corporate setting, a manager utilizes her emotional intelligence to mediate a heated dispute between two team members. She empathetically listens to both sides, acknowledges their emotions, and facilitates a resolution that addresses the concerns of all parties involved, thereby fostering a harmonious work environment.

Details:

In the realm of corporate conflict resolution, emotional intelligence plays a pivotal role in navigating and effectively resolving disputes. Consider the case of Sarah, a manager at a tech firm, faced with mediating a heated disagreement between two of her team members, Jack and Emma.

The conflict arose during a project meeting, where Jack, a senior developer, and Emma, a newer team member, clashed over the implementation strategy for a software feature. Tempers flared, and the meeting ended with unresolved tensions.

Sarah, recognizing the impact of this conflict on the team's morale and productivity, decided to intervene with a structured approach grounded in emotional intelligence. She first met with each team member individually to understand their perspectives and feelings. With Jack, she discovered underlying stressors related to his concerns about meeting project deadlines. Emma, on the other hand, felt her ideas were being dismissed due to her junior status.

In these individual sessions, Sarah practiced active listening, validating their emotions and concerns without immediately jumping to solutions.

This approach helped each team member feel heard and understood, a crucial step in conflict resolution.

Subsequently, Sarah arranged a joint meeting with both parties. She began by setting a tone of mutual respect and collaboration. Throughout the discussion, Sarah facilitated a balanced dialogue, encouraging empathy by asking Jack and Emma to consider each other's viewpoints. She guided them towards a common ground, focusing on the project's success rather than personal differences.

The outcome was a mutually agreed upon strategy that incorporated Emma's innovative ideas while addressing Jack's concerns about project timelines. Through her emotional intelligence, Sarah not only resolved the immediate conflict but also strengthened the team's ability to handle future disagreements constructively. Her approach fostered a more empathetic, understanding, and ultimately productive work environment.

2. EFFECTIVE COMMUNICATION:

A husband notices that his wife seems upset. Instead of dismissing her emotions or jumping to solutions, he employs active listening and empathetic understanding to explore her feelings. This open, non-judgmental communication fosters a deeper emotional connection and trust between them.

Details:

In a scenario involving effective communication, a husband recognizes his wife's distress. Instead of ignoring or hastily offering solutions, he adopts a thoughtful approach. He actively listens, showing genuine interest in understanding her perspective. He doesn't judge or interrupt, but rather encourages her to express her emotions freely. This empathetic listening helps uncover the root of her upset. Through this open and caring dialogue, they establish a stronger emotional bond. The husband's attentiveness not only soothes his wife's immediate distress but also builds a foundation of trust and deeper connection in their relationship, demonstrating the power of emotional intelligence in personal communication.

3. CUSTOMER SERVICE EXCELLENCE:

In a retail scenario, a customer service representative encounters an irate customer. Utilizing his emotional intelligence, he remains calm, acknowledges the customer's dissatisfaction, and works diligently to address the concern, turning a potentially negative experience into a positive one.

Details:

In a retail setting, a customer service representative faces a challenging situation with an angry customer. Applying his emotional intelligence skills, he maintains composure amidst the customer's frustration. He attentively listens to the customer, validating their feelings of dissatisfaction without taking the anger personally. Demonstrating empathy, he apologizes for the inconvenience and seeks to understand the root cause of the issue. With a solution-oriented mindset, he offers practical and satisfying resolutions, ensuring the customer feels heard and valued. His calm demeanor and proactive approach not only defuse the situation but also transform a potentially adverse experience into a positive one, leaving the customer feeling respected and well-serviced. This scenario exemplifies how emotional intelligence can be a crucial asset in customer service, turning challenging interactions into opportunities for excellent service and customer loyalty.

4. TEAM COLLABORATION:

A project leader harnesses EQ to foster a collaborative team environment. She is adept at recognizing and appreciating the diverse emotional and cognitive perspectives of team members, which cultivates a culture of respect, open communication, and collective problem-solving.

Details:

In a collaborative project, a team leader effectively utilizes her emotional intelligence (EQ) to cultivate a harmonious and productive team environment. She begins by recognizing the unique emotional states and cognitive styles of each team member, appreciating these differences as valuable assets. During team meetings, she encourages open communication, actively facilitating a platform where all voices are heard and respected. Her ability to empathize with her colleagues' perspectives helps in resolving misunderstandings and fostering mutual respect. By employing her EQ skills, she ensures that the team collaboratively approaches problem-solving, blending various viewpoints into innovative solutions. This inclusive and empathetic leadership approach not only enhances team dynamics but also drives creativity and efficiency, leading to successful project outcomes and a more engaged team.

5. PERSONAL RESILIENCE:

Following a personal setback, an individual employs EQ to process his emotions constructively. He acknowledges his disappointment, learns from the experience, and channels this insight into proactive steps towards future goals, demonstrating resilience and positive adaptation.

Details:

After experiencing a significant personal setback, John found himself grappling with a mix of disappointment and discouragement. However, instead of succumbing to these emotions, he decided to employ his emotional intelligence (EQ) skills to navigate through this challenging time. He started by openly acknowledging his feelings of disappointment, not shying away from or suppressing them. John then engaged in introspective analysis, examining what lessons the setback could offer. Through this process, he gained valuable insights into his strengths and areas for improvement. Gradually, he channeled this newfound understanding into formulating a plan for future endeavors, setting realistic and achievable goals. By facing his emotions head-on and learning from the experience, John demonstrated remarkable resilience. He adapted positively to the situation, transforming a potential negative spiral into a stepping stone for personal growth and future success.

6. LEADERSHIP INFLUENCE:

A CEO, through high emotional intelligence, creates a supportive organizational culture that values employee well-being and encourages feedback. His empathetic and authentic leadership style inspires loyalty, motivation, and enhanced performance among employees.

DETAILS:

In a thriving tech startup, CEO Emily leverages her high emotional intelligence to shape an organizational culture that deeply values employee well-being. Understanding the impact of leadership on team morale, she cultivates an environment where open communication and feedback are not just encouraged but celebrated. Emily regularly schedules one-on-one meetings with her team members, not only to discuss business objectives but also to genuinely inquire about their professional and personal well-being. Her empathetic approach to leadership creates a strong sense of trust and respect within the team.

She encourages her employees to voice their ideas and concerns, ensuring they feel heard and valued. This approach has fostered a sense of belonging and loyalty among the staff, who are more motivated and committed to the company's vision. Emily's authenticity in her interactions and decisions resonates with her team, inspiring them to perform at their best. Her leadership style not only drives high performance and innovation but also contributes to a positive and supportive workplace atmosphere. Employees often cite the company's culture and leadership as primary reasons for their job satisfaction and continued commitment to the organization's success.

7. NEGOTIATION MASTERY:

In a high-stakes negotiation, a skilled negotiator utilizes EQ to understand the underlying concerns and motivations of the other party. Through empathetic engagement and effective communication, she navigates towards a mutually beneficial agreement.

DETAILS:

In a tense boardroom setting, negotiator Sarah faces a high-stakes deal with a potential major client. The client, initially rigid in their demands, presents a challenging negotiation scenario. Sarah, equipped with her mastery of emotional intelligence (EQ), approaches the situation with a strategic blend of empathy and assertiveness.

Rather than countering their demands aggressively, she starts by actively listening to the client's concerns, picking up on subtle cues in their body language and tone. Sarah understands that behind their tough exterior, the client seeks assurance on quality and long-term support. She acknowledges these concerns directly, making the client feel understood and valued.

Sarah then skillfully redirects the conversation towards shared goals, emphasizing how her company's offerings align perfectly with the client's long-term objectives. She uses her EQ to maintain a calm and positive demeanor, diffusing any tension and creating an atmosphere conducive to open dialogue. Throughout the negotiation, Sarah balances her empathetic understanding with clear, assertive communication about her company's capabilities and limits. This approach helps her steer the conversation away from a deadlock and towards a win-win solution.

By the end of the session, the client, feeling heard and respected, agrees to a mutually beneficial arrangement. Sarah's ability to empathize, communicate effectively, and maintain emotional control under pressure not only secures a valuable deal for her company but also lays the foundation for a strong, ongoing business relationship.

8. COMMUNITY ENGAGEMENT:

A community leader leverages emotional intelligence to bridge diverse groups with varying interests. By fostering an environment of empathy, understanding, and respectful dialogue, he facilitates collaborative community initiatives that cater to the broader common good.

DETAILS:

In the diverse town of Harmonyville, community leader David faces the challenge of bridging gaps between various groups, each with distinct interests and backgrounds. David, known for his high emotional intelligence (EQ), steps into this role with a clear vision to foster unity and collaborative growth.

David begins by organizing a series of community meetings, inviting representatives from each group. These meetings are not just formal discussions but are designed as platforms for storytelling and shared experiences. David encourages participants to express their concerns, hopes, and visions for the community. He listens attentively, not just to words, but to the emotions behind them, demonstrating genuine empathy and under-standing.

Through these interactions, David identifies common grounds and mu-tual interests that often lie beneath surface-level differences. He proposes community projects that address these shared concerns, like a community garden that promotes environmental sustainability and provides a space for cultural exchange.

David's empathetic leadership fosters a sense of belonging and respect among the diverse groups. He mediates discussions with a calm and neu-tral stance, ensuring every voice is heard and valued. His ability to manage his own emotions and understand others' enables him to diffuse potential conflicts and steer conversations towards constructive outcomes.

Under David's guidance, Harmonyville sees the launch of several com-munity-driven initiatives. These projects not only cater to the broader common good but also strengthen the bonds between different communi-ty members. David's EQ-centric approach transforms Harmonyville into a model of inclusive and empathetic community engagement.

These real-world examples encapsulate the transformative potential of Emotional Intelligence across a myriad of life situations. From resolving conflicts and nurturing personal relationships to steering organizational success and fostering communal harmony, EQ emerges as an indispens-able asset. The practical manifestation of Emotional Intelligence show-cases its profound impact on enhancing interpersonal dynamics, resolving challenges, and cultivating a nurturing environment conducive to growth, understanding, and cooperative endeavor.

SUCCESS STORIES OF IMPROVED EQ

Let's delve into the transformative journeys of three individuals who harnessed the power of Emotional Intelligence (EQ) to reach new heights in their personal and professional lives. These real-life success stories illustrate the profound impact of developing EQ.

1. THE CORPORATE LEADER WHO LEARNED TO LISTEN:

John was a high-flying executive known for his sharp analytical skills and decisive nature. However, his climb up the corporate ladder stalled due to his abrasive management style. Feedback from his team highlighted a lack of empathy and poor listening skills. John took this to heart and began a journey to improve his EQ. He engaged in active listening exercises, took time to understand his emotions, and practiced empathy by putting himself in his colleagues' shoes. Over time, John's transformation was evident. He became a leader who inspired loyalty and creativity, leading his team to achieve record-breaking results. His company not only retained key talent but became a leader in employee satisfaction.

2. THE TEACHER WHO TURNED EMPATHY INTO ACTION:

Sarah, a middle school teacher, struggled to connect with her students, which reflected in their performance and engagement. After attending a workshop on Emotional Intelligence, she realized that she had been approaching her students as a collective rather than as individuals with unique emotional needs. Sarah began to incorporate empathy in her teaching methods, giving special attention to each student's emotional state. She created a classroom environment where students felt seen and understood. This led to a marked improvement in class participation, academic performance, and a drop in behavioral issues. Sarah's empathetic approach turned her classroom into a nurturing environment for learning.

3. THE ENTREPRENEUR WHO MASTERED SELF-REGULATION:

Alex, an entrepreneur, was passionate but impulsive, often letting stress dictate his business decisions. After a particularly rash decision resulted in a significant loss, Alex decided to focus on developing his EQ, particularly self-regulation. He learned stress-reduction techniques, such as meditation and mindful breathing, and applied these before making business decisions. Alex also cultivated a habit of reflecting on his emotions and the underlying reasons for them. This allowed him to approach business challenges with a clear and composed mind, leading to better decision-making. His startup not only recovered from the previous setback but thrived, attracting investors and earning a reputation for its innovative and thoughtful leadership.

Each of these stories underscores a facet of EQ - be it empathy, self-awareness, or self-regulation - and showcases how it can be a game-changer. These individuals exemplify that while the journey to enhancing EQ is deeply personal, the benefits extend far beyond the self, positively impacting everyone around us. Their stories serve as motivation for anyone looking to enhance their emotional intelligence and thereby, their success in life.

CHAPTER 8
SELF-ASSESSMENT & RELAXATION TECHNIQUES

Let's delve into the intricate balance of understanding oneself and finding inner tranquility. This chapter guides you through introspective practices and relaxation methods, essential for cultivating a deeper sense of self-awareness and peace. Embrace this journey towards personal clarity and serenity, as we explore tools to assess and soothe your mind and emotions.

EQ TEST: EVALUATE YOUR EMOTIONAL INTELLIGENCE

This test is designed to help you assess your Emotional Intelligence (EQ). For each question, choose the answer that best describes your usual behavior or feeling. Each answer has a score, which will be used to determine your EQ profile.

1. WHEN FACED WITH A STRESSFUL SITUATION, YOU USUALLY:

- A. Feel overwhelmed and avoid it (1 point)
- B. Get anxious but face it anyway (2 points)
- C. Stay calm and assess the situation rationally (4 points)
- D. Seek help or advice from others (3 points)
- E. Try to distract yourself from it (1 point)

2. WHEN SOMEONE DISAGREES WITH YOU, YOU:

- A. Feel personally attacked (1 point)
- B. Try to understand their point of view (4 points)
- C. Insist on your own perspective (2 points)
- D. Avoid further discussion (1 point)
- E. Seek a compromise (3 points)

3. HOW DO YOU HANDLE CRITICISM?

- A. Get defensive and justify your actions (2 points)
- B. Feel hurt but don't show it (1 point)
- C. Reflect on it to understand and improve (4 points)
- D. Ignore it (1 point)
- E. Take it constructively and ask for more feedback (3 points)

4. WHEN YOU'RE FEELING DOWN:

- A. You don't know why (1 point)
- B. You analyze the reasons behind it (4 points)
- C. You try to shake it off with activities (2 points)
- D. Talk to someone about it (3 points)
- E. Dwell on negative thoughts (1 point)

5. IN A TEAM, YOU:

- A. Prefer to follow others' leads (2 points)
- B. Encourage open discussion and collaboration (4 points)
- C. Often take charge of the situation (3 points)
- D. Avoid participating (1 point)
- E. Focus only on your part (2 points)

6. WHEN SOMEONE SHARES A PROBLEM WITH YOU, YOU:

- A. Offer solutions immediately (3 points)
- B. Listen, but feel unsure how to respond (2 points)
- C. Empathize and share similar experiences (4 points)
- D. Change the subject to avoid discomfort (1 point)
- E. Encourage them to solve it on their own (2 points)

7. IN A HEATED ARGUMENT, YOU:

- A. Tend to raise your voice and get emotional (1 point)
- B. Stay calm and try to reason (4 points)
- C. Withdraw or walk away from the situation (2 points)
- D. Focus on finding a middle ground (3 points)
- E. Often give in to avoid conflict (2 points)

8. HOW DO YOU HANDLE FAILURE OR SETBACKS?

- A. Blame external factors (1 point)

- B. Reflect on what went wrong and plan to improve (4 points)
- C. Feel discouraged and lose motivation (1 point)
- D. Seek feedback and take constructive action (3 points)
- E. Move on quickly without much thought (2 points)

9. WHEN WORKING ON A GROUP PROJECT, YOU:

- A. Wait for others to take the lead (2 points)
- B. Make sure everyone's opinions are heard (4 points)
- C. Push your ideas strongly (3 points)
- D. Prefer to work alone (1 point)
- E. Compromise often to maintain harmony (3 points)

10. IF SOMEONE IS UPSET, YOU:

- A. Feel uncomfortable and distance yourself (1 point)
- B. Try to cheer them up with humor (2 points)
- C. Listen and provide emotional support (4 points)
- D. Offer logical solutions to their problems (3 points)
- E. Get affected and feel upset yourself (2 points)

11. WHEN YOU'RE GIVEN A COMPLIMENT, YOU:

- A. Feel embarrassed and dismiss it (1 point)
- B. Appreciate it and say thank you (3 points)
- C. Wonder if it's genuine (2 points)
- D. Feel proud and agree (2 points)
- E. Reflect on your strengths and areas for improvement (4 points)

12. HOW DO YOU APPROACH PERSONAL GOALS AND CHALLENGES?

- A. Avoid them due to fear of failure (1 point)
- B. Set realistic goals and work steadily towards them (4 points)
- C. Get excited but lose focus over time (2 points)

- D. Seek advice and support from others (3 points)
- E. Tend to overcommit and feel overwhelmed (2 points)

13. WHEN MAKING DECISIONS, YOU:
- A. Rely heavily on others' opinions (2 points)
- B. Analyze all possible outcomes before deciding (4 points)
- C. Go with your gut feeling (3 points)
- D. Procrastinate and struggle to decide (1 point)
- E. Make quick decisions without much thought (2 points)

14. HOW DO YOU FEEL ABOUT CHANGE?
- A. Resist and prefer routine (1 point)
- B. Adapt easily and see it as an opportunity (4 points)
- C. Feel anxious but try to cope (3 points)
- D. Accept it but feel unsettled (2 points)
- E. Seek change regularly for excitement (3 points)

15. WHEN COMMUNICATING WITH OTHERS, YOU:
- A. Often find it hard to express your thoughts (1 point)
- B. Speak clearly and listen actively (4 points)
- C. Tend to talk about yourself a lot (2 points)
- D. Adjust your communication style to suit the listener (3 points)
- E. Prefer to communicate through actions rather than words (2 points)

16. HOW DO YOU HANDLE CRITICISM?
- A. Get defensive and argue (1 point)
- B. Reflect on it and seek to improve (4 points)
- C. Feel upset but don't show it (2 points)
- D. Accept it graciously and thank the person (3 points)
- E. Ignore it and don't let it affect you (2 points)

17. WHEN YOU'RE STRESSED, YOU:

- A. Tend to shut down and withdraw (2 points)
- B. Look for healthy ways to relax and recharge (4 points)
- C. Focus on solving the problem causing stress (3 points)
- D. Get irritable and snap at others (1 point)
- E. Seek support from friends or family (3 points)

18. IN SOCIAL SITUATIONS, YOU:

- A. Feel nervous and prefer to observe (2 points)
- B. Easily engage and interact with others (4 points)
- C. Try to dominate conversations (1 point)
- D. Listen more than you speak (3 points)
- E. Enjoy being the center of attention (2 points)

19. HOW DO YOU APPROACH TEAM CONFLICTS?

- A. Avoid getting involved (2 points)
- B. Act as a mediator to resolve issues (4 points)
- C. Focus on your viewpoint only (1 point)
- D. Seek a compromise that satisfies everyone (3 points)
- E. Feel stressed and hope it resolves on its own (2 points)

20. WHEN YOU HAVE FREE TIME, YOU:

- A. Engage in hobbies or activities you enjoy (3 points)
- B. Reflect on your personal growth and goals (4 points)
- C. Spend time with friends and family (3 points)
- D. Worry about things you need to do (2 points)
- E. Prefer not to plan and take things as they come (2 points)

RANGE	EQ LEVEL	DESCRIPTION
15 - 30	Emerging EQ	You are beginning to understand your emotions and those of others but might struggle in managing and expressing them effectively.
31 - 45	Developing EQ	You show awareness of emotions and some ability to handle interpersonal relations judiciously and empathetically.
46 - 60	Competent EQ	You exhibit a good understanding of emotions, their impact, and use this understanding effectively in your interactions.
61 - 75	Advanced EQ	You possess high emotional intelligence, demonstrating a strong ability to manage emotions, both yours and others', to foster positive relationships.
> 76	Masterful EQ	You excel in understanding and managing emotions, using this mastery to achieve personal and professional success while helping others.

Remember, this test is a general guide and not a definitive measurement of emotional intelligence. Developing EQ is a continuous process, and there are always opportunities for growth and improvement.

MINDFULNESS AND RELAXATION TECHNIQUES

In the fast-paced world we live in, stress and anxiety have become common companions, affecting our emotional intelligence (EQ) and overall well-being. Mindfulness and relaxation techniques are vital tools that can enhance our EQ by fostering self-awareness, reducing stress, and improving our ability to respond rather than react in challenging situations.

1. THE ESSENCE OF MINDFULNESS:

Mindfulness is a mental state achieved by focusing one's awareness on the present moment. It involves acknowledging and accepting one's feelings, thoughts, and bodily sensations. Regular mindfulness practice enhances emotional regulation and self-awareness, core components of EQ.

Practical Exercise: The Mindful Moment

Take a few minutes each day to sit quietly. Focus on your breath, observing the rise and fall of your chest and the sensation of air entering and leaving your nostrils. If your mind wanders, gently bring it back to your breath. This practice helps anchor you in the present, increasing your awareness of your emotional state.

2. DEEP BREATHING TECHNIQUES:

Stress and anxiety often manifest through rapid, shallow breathing. Deep breathing exercises can counteract this by activating the body's natural relaxation response.

Practical Exercise: Breathing Techniques:

Complete Breathing

Breathing is the rhythm of life, and full, deep breathing is like a symphony in its entirety. Such breathing practices involve the whole respiratory system, filling every part of us with life-giving oxygen and energy. Through the practice of full breathing, we create a symphony between our physical and mental selves, understanding that each breath in and out is a link to the cosmos.

* Exercise Time for each series: 5-7 breath cycles
* Exercise Series Number: 3
* Exercise Total Time: Variable
* Trained Area: Respiratory system, relaxation

Instructions:

* Find a comfortable seated or lying position.
* Inhale deeply through your nose, expanding your belly, then your ribcage, and finally filling your chest.
* Exhale completely through your mouth, emptying your chest, ribcage, and belly.
* Continue this cycle of deep inhalation and exhalation, focusing on the rhythm of your breath.
* With each breath, invite relaxation and a sense of renewal.

Chinese Breathing

Drawing on the profound insights of ancient traditions, Chinese breathing exercises blend breath and movement to foster inner harmony and energy. These techniques honor the dynamic flow of life force within, steering us towards equilibrium and wellness. In practicing Chinese breathing methods, we connect with time-honored wisdom, weaving these practices into our contemporary quest for comprehensive health.

* Exercise Time for each series: 5-7 breath cycles
* Exercise Series Number: 3
* Exercise Total Time: Variable
* Trained Area: Energy channels, relaxation

Instructions:

- Stand or sit comfortably with your back straight.
- Inhale deeply through your nose as you raise your arms out to your sides and above your head.
- Exhale slowly through your mouth as you lower your arms back down.
- Coordinate your breath with the arm movements, focusing on the flow of energy.
- Embrace the sensation of energy circulating through your body with each breath and movement.

Diaphragmatic Breathing

The diaphragm plays a crucial, yet often unnoticed role in the orchestration of our breathing. By engaging in diaphragmatic breathing exercises, we enhance our lung capacity and usher in a state of relaxation, allowing the diaphragm to perform its vital function effectively. Through this practice, we delve into the nuances of our breathing, acknowledging that each inhale and exhale enriches both our physical being and our inner essence.

- Exercise Time for each series: 5-7 breath cycles
- Exercise Series Number: 3
- Exercise Total Time: Variable
- Trained Area: Diaphragm, relaxation

Instructions:

- Find a comfortable seated or lying position.
- Place one hand on your chest and the other on your belly.
- Inhale deeply through your nose, allowing your belly to rise as you fill your lungs.
- Exhale slowly through your mouth, feeling your belly lower as you release the breath.

- Focus on the sensation of your diaphragm moving with each breath, embracing the rhythm of relaxation.

Buteyko Breathing

Buteyko breathing exercises are centered on cultivating mindful breath awareness and control, tapping into the innate intelligence of our bodies. They emphasize the importance of decelerating our breathing rhythm, fostering a state of relaxation, and enhancing our oxygen uptake. Through the practice of Buteyko breathing, we celebrate the mindful art of breathing, acknowledging each breath as a precious offering of life and energy.

- Exercise Time for each series: 5-7 breath cycles
- Exercise Series Number: 3
- Exercise Total Time: Variable
- Trained Area: Breath control, relaxation

Instructions:

- Find a comfortable seated or lying position.
- Inhale gently through your nose for a count of 2.
- Exhale slowly through your nose for a count of 4.
- Continue this cycle of gentle inhalation and slow exhalation, focusing on the rhythm.
- Embrace the tranquility that comes with conscious breath, allowing it to guide you into a state of relaxation.

3. PROGRESSIVE MUSCLE RELAXATION (PMR):

PMR involves gradually tensing and then relaxing different muscle groups in the body. This technique is effective in reducing physical tension and associated mental stress.

Practical Exercise: Tense and Release

Start at your feet and work your way up to your head. Tense each muscle group for five seconds and then relax for 30 seconds. Pay attention to the sensation of release in each muscle. This exercise is particularly beneficial before bedtime to alleviate insomnia linked to stress.

4. GUIDED IMAGERY:

Guided imagery is a relaxation technique that involves visualizing a peaceful scene or situation. It utilizes the power of the mind to induce calm.

Practical Exercise: Visualization

Close your eyes and imagine a serene place – a beach, a forest, or a garden. Visualize the details – the sounds, the smells, the colors. Engage all your senses to make the experience vivid. This mental escape can provide a quick respite from stress.

5. MINDFUL MOVEMENT PRACTICES:

Yoga, Tai Chi, and Qigong combine physical postures, breathing techniques, and meditation. They are excellent for reducing stress and enhancing bodily awareness.

Practical Exercise: Yoga and Tai Chi

Incorporate basic yoga poses or Tai Chi movements into your routine. Focus on the flow of movements and your breath, which creates a meditative state, fostering both physical and mental relaxation.

6. MEDITATION AND CONTEMPLATIVE PRACTICES:

Meditation involves training the mind to focus and redirect thoughts. It can increase self-awareness, reduce negative emotions, and enhance concentration and attention.

Practical Exercise: Daily Meditation

Dedicate a few minutes each day to meditation. You can use apps or guid-ed meditation videos as a starting point. Focus on your breath or a mantra, allowing your mind to become more centered and peaccful.

In Conclusion:

Incorporating these mindfulness and relaxation techniques into your daily life can significantly enhance your EQ. They lead to better stress man-agement, heightened self-awareness, and improved emotional regulation. Over time, these practices contribute to more meaningful interactions, better relationships, and an overall enhanced quality of life. Remember, the journey to high EQ is continuous, and these practices can be integral tools in navigating this path.

CONCLUSION

As we reach the conclusion of our exploration into the art of Emotional Intelligence (EQ), it's important to reflect on the profound journey we have undertaken. Emotional Intelligence is not merely a set of skills or an academic concept; it is a transformative approach to life. It influences how we perceive ourselves, interact with others, make decisions, and navigate the complexities of human emotions. This journey through the realms of self-awareness, self-regulation, motivation, empathy, and social skills has illuminated the myriad ways in which EQ enhances our personal and professional lives.

THE INTEGRATIVE POWER OF EQ

The exploration of EQ begins with an inward journey, understanding and managing our own emotions. It's about recognizing our emotional triggers and learning how to respond, rather than react. This self-awareness is the foundation upon which other EQ skills are built. It enables us to regulate our emotions, keeping impulsivity and negative reactions in check. By mastering self-regulation, we gain control over our responses, leading to more constructive outcomes in challenging situations.

EQ IN INTERPERSONAL RELATIONSHIPS

Moving beyond ourselves, EQ is invaluable in understanding and empathizing with others. It allows us to step into someone else's shoes, appreciate their perspectives, and respond with sensitivity and awareness. This ability is crucial in both personal relationships and professional environments. It fosters deeper connections, improves communication, and facilitates conflict resolution. Through empathy and social skills, EQ empowers us to build robust networks, nurture lasting relationships, and become more effective leaders.

THE ROLE OF EQ IN PROFESSIONAL SUCCESS

In the workplace, EQ is a key determinant of success. It goes beyond technical skills and intellectual prowess. Emotionally intelligent professionals are better equipped to handle pressures and stresses of the corporate world. They make more informed, empathetic decisions, understand team dynamics, and lead with inspiration. EQ in leadership transcends the traditional authoritarian model, advocating a more inclusive, empathetic approach that resonates deeply with employees, thereby fostering a more positive and productive work environment.

EQ FOR PERSONAL FULFILLMENT

On a personal level, EQ contributes significantly to mental health and overall well-being. It helps in managing stress, anxiety, and depression, promoting a more balanced and fulfilling life. Emotionally intelligent individuals enjoy stronger relationships, have a greater understanding of themselves, and navigate life's ups and downs with resilience and grace.

THE CONTINUOUS JOURNEY OF EQ DEVELOPMENT

It's crucial to acknowledge that EQ is not a destination but a journey. It is a continuous process of learning, practicing, and growing. The landscape of our emotions and relationships is ever-changing, and our EQ skills must evolve accordingly. Regular self-reflection, openness to feedback, and a commitment to personal growth are essential for maintaining and enhancing our emotional intelligence.

EQ AND THE FUTURE

Looking ahead, the importance of EQ is only set to increase. In a world that is rapidly changing and increasingly interconnected, the ability to navigate emotional landscapes will be more critical than ever. From fostering global collaborations to leading with compassion, EQ will be at the forefront of shaping a more empathetic and understanding world.

EMBRACING EQ IN EVERYDAY LIFE

As we conclude, it's important to embrace EQ in our daily lives. It's about being mindful of our emotions and those of others, practicing empathy, and making conscious efforts to improve our emotional skills. Whether in personal relationships, professional environments, or individual pursuits,

EQ is a powerful tool that can lead to a more fulfilling, balanced, and successful life.

FINAL THOUGHTS

In summary, the art of Emotional Intelligence is about understanding and mastering the complex world of emotions. It's about using this understanding to live more harmoniously with ourselves and others. As we continue to navigate the nuances of EQ, let's remember that every step taken in improving our emotional intelligence is a step towards a more insightful, compassionate, and fulfilling life.

EQ SEDUCTION & LAWS OF ATTRACTION

The Laws of Attraction, much like gravity, is an ever-present force in our lives, shaping our reality based on the vibrations we emit. This concept hinges on understanding the complex relationship between our mind and body. Our body, a dynamic field of energy, remains in motion throughout our existence, reflecting the profound impact of our thoughts and emotions.

The mind is divided into conscious and subconscious realms. The subconscious mind, formed from early experiences and inherited beliefs, holds paradigms that deeply influence our life. These paradigms, a blend of habits and beliefs, often override our conscious thoughts and dictate the vibrational frequency of our existence, thus shaping the reality we experience.

The essence of the Law of Attraction is not merely in positive thinking but in aligning our subconscious paradigms with our conscious desires. This alignment necessitates a transformation not just in thought, but at a deeper emotional and subconscious level. Our emotional responses, shaped by these paradigms, significantly influence the vibrations we emit and, in turn, the experiences we attract.

Emotional intelligence (EQ) plays a pivotal role in this process. It involves becoming aware of and regulating our emotions, empathizing with others, and managing relationships effectively. By harnessing EQ, we can consciously influence our vibrations, aligning them with our desired outcomes.

This chapter reveals that to alter our reality, we must first shift the emotional and subconscious frequencies at which we operate. EQ becomes a powerful tool in tuning our vibrations to attract positive experiences, leading us towards fulfillment and success. The journey of mastering the Laws of Attraction is thus deeply intertwined with developing and applying emotional intelligence.

In a world brimming with self-help mantras and manifestation guides, the confluence of emotional intelligence and the laws of attraction creates a powerful nexus for personal growth. This bonus chapter explores this intriguing intersection, unraveling how a deep understanding of one's emotional landscape can attract life's myriad bounties.

THE ESSENCE OF EMOTIONAL CLARITY

At the heart of emotional intelligence lies clarity. It's the sharp image that emerges from the fog of our complex emotional atmospheres. This clarity isn't solely about discerning our feelings but extends to understanding the intricate dance of cause and effect in our interactions. Why are we drawn into certain situations? What lessons are woven into the fabric of these encounters? These are the questions that a person with high emotional intelligence ponders, seeking not just to react but to understand and grow.

THE MAGNETIC PULL OF THOUGHTS AND FEELINGS

The laws of attraction hinge on a simple yet profound principle: like attracts like. It's not just about positive thinking or visualizing success; it's about the powerful current that runs beneath - our emotions. Consider the image of a chimpanzee in a pinstripe suit; despite instructions to the contrary, it persists in the mind's eye because it's tied to the emotional reaction it provokes. In this light, the laws of attraction aren't about superficial desires but the deeper emotional vibrations that resonate within us.

MANIFESTING THROUGH EMOTIONAL FOCUS

Life's clutter often distracts from the heart's true desires. The dusty exercise equipment and abandoned diets are testaments to misaligned intentions. The key to harnessing the laws of attraction lies in a concerted focus on our genuine emotional desires. What we persistently think and feel, we bring into being. This realization calls for a vigilant monitoring of our internal emotional dialogues. Are we nurturing seeds of negativity, or are we cultivating a garden of positive aspirations?

THE UNSEEN BLUEPRINT OF REALITY

Everything tangible was once intangible, a mere whisper of thought before it was birthed into reality. This is the playground of emotional intelligence, where we call forth the unseen into the seen. However, the act of creation isn't a conscious endeavor; it's a subconscious symphony. The subconscious mind, often overlooked, is the true architect of our reality. It operates in the background, driving our actions and outcomes, much like the automatic journey home that we don't consciously recall.

NAVIGATING THE MOMENT WITH INTENTION

The present moment is a fertile ground for emotional intelligence to manifest the laws of attraction. It's in the 'now' that we can tune into the subtle whispers of opportunity and purpose. When irritations arise, they're not merely annoyances but mirrors reflecting back parts of ourselves that require attention and growth. By engaging with the present, by being proactive rather than reactive, we open ourselves to the teachings that each moment offers.

MEDITATION: THE QUIET POWER

In the stillness lies the answer. Meditation, stripped of any esoteric connotations, is simply about silence, about creating a space where our circumstances can resonate with the core of our being. It's in this quietude that our true desires can make themselves known, untainted by the cacophony of daily existence. This emotional resonance acts as a guide, steering us toward what feels right and true, even if it makes sense only to us.

THE PURSUIT OF GREATER TRUTH

In the quest for self-realization, it's essential to differentiate facts from truth. Facts are the terrain of our reality, but truth is the compass that guides us through it. Seeking a greater truth is an act of courage, an inward journey that confronts fears, societal norms, and our own limitations. It's in this confrontation that emotional intelligence merges with the laws of attraction, igniting a passion and purpose that propels us forward.

THE LEAP OF FAITH AND THE PROMISE OF ALIGNMENT

Just as a football player doesn't wait for the ball to arrive before running, we too must move toward our goals with faith. Our belief in the outcome, coupled with our emotional conviction, sets the stage for receiving what we seek. For what we long for with our hearts is simultaneously reaching out to us, in a cosmic dance of attraction and manifestation.

THE ESSENTIAL PLAN B

In the intricate dance of emotional intelligence, seduction, and the laws of attraction, a nuanced understanding of human interactions becomes pivotal. It's here that the concept of having a "Plan B" and engaging in multiple flirtations emerges not as a strategy of deceit, but as a testament to self-awareness and emotional agility. This approach underscores the importance of not placing all emotional investments into a single interaction, thereby maintaining a sense of balance and objectivity. When one is too deeply engrossed in a single flirtation, it's easy to lose sight of rationality, allowing emotions to cloud judgment. This intense focus can lead to idealization, where perceived connections or rejections disproportionately impact one's self-esteem and decision-making processes. Emotional intelligence in this realm involves recognizing the transient nature of attractions and interactions, and the value in diversifying one's emotional portfolio.

Engaging with multiple interests simultaneously allows an individual to better navigate the social landscape, learning from a variety of interactions to refine their understanding of personal desires and boundaries. It fosters a detachment that is not cold or uncaring, but rather, pragmatically affectionate - acknowledging the fleeting nature of most connections while still valuing their depth and potential for growth.

Moreover, a "Plan B" or multiple flirtations serve as a reminder that one's value and emotional fulfillment do not hinge on a single outcome. This strategy enhances resilience, ensuring that one's emotional well-being is not irrevocably tied to the whims of attraction but is instead rooted in a self-assured, balanced understanding of interpersonal dynamics.

In this journey, emotional intelligence is the compass, and the laws of attraction, the map. Together, they chart a course to a life where every challenge is an opportunity, every emotion a teacher, and every desire a beacon drawing us ever closer to our truest selves.

Made in the USA
Las Vegas, NV
26 November 2024

12679105R00077